The Ultimate Filmmaking Term Pocketbook Glossary

USHER MORGAN

Published by:
Library Tales Publishing
www.LibraryTalesPublishing.com
www.Facebook.com/LibraryTalesPublishing

ISBN-13: 978-1-956769-59-3

Table of Contents

WELCOME

Welcome to *The Ultimate Filmmaking Term Pocketbook Glossary - From A to Z: Unlocking the Language of Filmmaking.* This pocket-sized glossary contains over 2,000 essential filmmaking terms used on-set, during pre-production, post-production, and throughout the film industry's creative and business communities.

Whether you're a budding filmmaker, an aspiring film producer, an actor in training, or just a cinema enthusiast eager to learn the lingo of filmmaking, this pocket-sized book is the tool for you! After all, it's best not to look like a cold brick on your first day on set. What's a "cold brick," you ask? Dive in to find out! (it's under 'C,' just in case you were wondering.)

So grab your copy, slip it into your pocket, and get ready to make some movie magic happen!

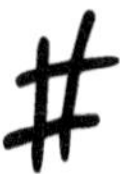

1 and 2 (A and B). Used to refer to the first and second mark of a camera move. Meaning you move the camera from point 1 (A) to point 2 (B). This can also refer to actor marks for their blocking positions during a scene. "Go back to one!" is a common term on-set meaning all parties return to starting positions.

1.25:1. The classic 5:4 aspect ratio of yesteryear's computer monitors. It may be old school, but it's got charm and personality like no other.

1.33:1, 4:3. A boxy aspect ratio format used in early film and television. Also known as the 4:3, this aspect ratio is mostly used today by filmmakers for artistic purposes, because old stuff is awesome!

1.375:1. Also known as the "Academy Ratio", another boxy aspect ratio used in old, 35mm film before the popularization of widescreen. The 1.375:1 was standardized in 1932 by the Academy of Motion Picture Arts and Sciences. It got a recent boost in popularity a few years after Wes Anderson was born.

1.43:1. A massive 70mm IMAX film aspect ratio format. It's big, awesome, and you can't afford it!

1.6:1. The 16:10 (or 8:5) ratio used in PC displays before the popularization of the vastly superior 16:9.

1.77:1, 16:9. The most common wide-screen aspect ratio format. If aspect ratio were a popularity content, 16:9 would take the cake!

1.85:1. The OG widescreen cinema aspect ratio. When cinema attendance dropped, Universal Studios created a widescreen aspect ratio for the release of 1953's *Thunder Bay* in order to pull audiences away from their boxy TV screens.

10 Bit. The number of color levels available in a digital signal. The higher the number of bits, the more vivid the picture and more room to play during color grading. In short, your colorist will thank you!

10-1. A cast or crew member left the set to pee, "going number 1." Called over the walkies.

10-2. A cast or crew member left the set to poop, "going number 2." May be called *loudly* over the walkies for *everyone* on set to hear. Better look into that crafty. #Nojudgement.

10-3. A cast or crew member hit the 'porcelain throne' and is sick in the bathroom. Called over the walkies. In case you thought there's privacy on set…

10-4!, Copy. Message understood, loud and clear.

10-T Driver. Think you're a big shot? Try maneuvering a 10-ton grip truck. A right reserved to 10-T Teamster Drivers.

1080. A frequently used HD resolution of 1920x1080. Also known as the 1080p. Bet you knew that already…

15mm rods. Think of these as the camera rig's wingmen, helping to mount all the cool accessories onto your camera setup. And yes, you'll need to know what a "rig" is too.

180 Degree Rule. A filmmaking guideline for the camera's position in a dialogue scene where the characters are facing each other. In a nutshell, characters should always have the same left to right relationship with each other. If Actor A is facing right, then Actor B should be facing left. Otherwise, you risk Janet looking at Bill, and Bill looking back at Bill. It wouldn't make any sense!

1st/2nd Assistant Editor. Editing room assistant responsible for providing logistical assistance to the editor and making sure they remember where 'finalproject_9471.prj" is located.

1st AD, 1st/First Assistant Director. The right-hand of the film's director, ensuring the set runs smoothly and that everyone knows what they're supposed to do on the day and how long we have till lunch. They are easily identifiable on set due to their signature binder, walkie-talkie, and anxious demeanor.

1st Camera Assist, 1st AC, Focus Puller. Camera crew member responsible for assisting the camera operator. They pull focus, swap lenses, and assist the camera operator in general. They're the ones keeping things in focus, so... pay and feed them well or risk having to constantly squint at the dang monitor wondering if you need a new pair of glasses.

2-Pop. A one-frame long, 1 kHz tone used to ensure sync between sound and picture.

2.3/3.2 Pulldown. The post-production process of converting 24 FPS film to 29.97 FPS, typically for the purpose of complying with international broadcasting standards.

2.39:1, 2.35:1, 2.40:1, 2.55:1. Wide anamorphic aspect ratios for you wide-screen lovers out there.

20, What's Your 20? "What is your location?" Spoken over the Walkies, often by a crew member or a perturbed AD.

24 fps, 24 frames-per-second. The standard frame rate for film, used in every movie you've ever seen (with some unfortunate, notable exceptions #NotMyHobbit)

2nd 2nd Assistant Director. An assistant to the 2nd Assistant Director. Often responsible for handling extras and screaming at pedestrians on set.

2nd AD. See Second Assistant Director.

2nd Camera Assist, 2nd AC, Clapper Loader. An assistant to the assistant cameraman, because the assistant needs an assistant too! Also known for loading the raw film stock, operating the clapperboard, marking the actors, and maintaining the Camera Log. They're busy people, clearly.

3-Point Edit. A film editing technique where one adds a clip into a timeline track by setting three edit points: (1) in; (2) out; and (3) the point in the timeline where the new clip is being added.

3-Point Lighting. The standard method used to light a scene by using three separate lights: Key Light, Fill Light and Backlight. Or in short, Key, Back, Fill.

3,200K. The color temperature of tungsten light. The K stands for Kelvin. 3,200K produces a warm yellow color, often used to replicate and match practical lights. Watch *Barry Lyndon*, you'll get it.

3D. A stereoscopic technology that creates the illusion of three-dimensional depth. Popularized in the 50s with the release of the masterpiece *Bwana Devil*, and faded in popularity when audiences realized that the only filmmaker capable of 3D worth paying extra for is James Cameron.

3DS-Max. Software for computer animation and VFX; great for making particle effects, modeling and rendering photorealistic shots that aren't as photorealistic as you'd like them to be.

4:2:2. A professional digital color sampling rate. It allows colorists to color-correct and grade footage with minimal data loss, as well as maximize use of green screen and VFX awesomeness.

4:3. A boxy aspect ratio format used in early film and television.

4.4.4. An uncompressed digital color sampling rate providing more color information than 4.2.2. Luminance and color data are transported in their purest form, ready to save your shot and to cost you a fortune in extra hard drives.

480p. A resolution of either 720x480 or 704x480 pixels. Either way, it's not enough. Buy a better camera!

48fps. An experimental high frame-rate responsible for making Middle Earth look like a video game in The *Hobbit*.

4K. A term used to describe high resolution footage with horizontal resolution of approximately 4,000 pixels.

5-T Driver. A Teamsters Union Driver licensed to drive a five-ton grip truck, because when you try to drive one yourself, bad/hilarious things will happen.

5,400K. Daylight color temperature. 5,400K produces a colder white color, often used to replicate fluorescent lights.

5.1 Channel Digital Sound. A surround sound audio system commonly used in that home theater room your dad's been trying to build since 2007. The "5" in 5.1 refers to the number of main audio channels that the format uses, which are typically front left, front right, center, rear left, and rear right. The ".1" refers to the subwoofer channel, which handles low-frequency sounds such as bass and drums. Together, these six channels create a spatial and immersive audio experience that can make the listener feel like they are in the middle of the action, fighting alongside John Wick to avenge the dog that died 4 movies ago!

555. A phone number shown on-screen typically starts with "555", it's an exchange number reserved for use by TV shows and movies, created by phone companies to put an end to pesky pranks and "intelligent people" calling up fictional characters for some reason.

7.1 Surround Sound. An eight-channel surround audio system adding two additional speakers to the 5.1 Channel Digital Sound configuration.

You're welcome.

70/30 Deal. A film distribution deal in which the distributor recoups pre-defined expenses *first* before splitting the balance 70/30. 70% goes to the distributor and 30% to the producer. You will sign it, and you will like it.

720p. A "high-definition" resolution of 1280x720 pixels used in high-def televisions. I added sarcastic quotes around the term, "high-definition," a meaningless marketing term used since the '30s.

8 Bit. The number of color levels available in older digital signals. A step up from 1-bit but still a long way from 16-bit. One day, you'll get there!

86. To "86" something means to remove or get rid of it. The term "strike" is also commonly used in the same context. For instance, you might say "86 the dolly", or "Tell the set dresser to strike those damn alien skulls." God, we love filmmaking!

8mm, Standard-8, Double 8, Super 8. A film format that's 8 millimeters wide and was introduced by Kodak during the Great Depression as an affordable alternative to 16mm and 35mm. Super 8 was later added to the lineup and made amateur filmmaking more accessible and of "higher quality." This format revolutionized the amateur film community and continues to be used to this day. It's "the little engine that could" of the filmmaking world, and it's pretty as hell!!

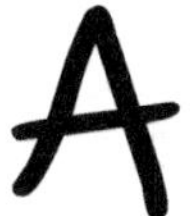

A-List. The coveted group of Hollywood elites who have the power to bring in the big bucks at the box office. Being an A-Lister means your name on the poster is enough to get people to buy tickets, it also means you get all the green M&Ms you want!

A.D Converter, ADC, Analog-to-Digital Converter. A digital system that takes analog signals (e.g. old-school Betamax tapes) and transforms them into the language of the digital age (mouthwatering 8k Imax footage).

A/B roll(s). Two or more rolls of captured footage. A-roll refers to the main footage or shots captured, while B-roll is considered "alternative" footage. This can include inserts, FX, establishing shots, stock footage, pickup shots, and BTS of actors throwing tantrums when they think no one's recording.

A24. The indie production company that's been making waves in the film world with its roster of critically-acclaimed hits including *Hereditary*, *Moonlight*, and *Everything Everywhere All at Once*.

Abby Singer. The Abby Singer is the second-to-last shot of the day. Named after the renowned production manager Abby Singer. Not to be confused with the Martini Shot, which is the actual last shot of the day.

Aberration, Lens Aberrations. An image distortion or unique color effect created due to a flaw in the lens. It adds character and style and can look awesome, in the right context. It can also be re-created in VFX to make people think you shot your film on vintage lenses #FakeItTillYouMakeIt

Above The Line, ATL. In film budgets, the term is used to represent the "big shots" as well as the "cream of the crop" expenses. This includes the cost to hire the director, writer(s), producers, principal cast, and other high-level creative personnel. The rest of the expenses, such as crew, catering, and gimbals that never work, are considered "below the line."

Above the Title. The names of actors, key producers and other VIP's displayed before the movie's title comes across the screen. It's the most coveted credit in the movie industry, second only to the highly sought after "Assistant to Mr. Gibson" credit.

Abstract. A genre of film where the audience is thrown into the strange mind of the filmmaker; anything is possible, and everything is up for interpretation. Whether you find it confusing, thought-provoking, strangely arousing, or just plain weird, an abstract film is guaranteed to leave you with a memorable viewing experience. Famous examples include *Atlantis*, 2013's *Visitors*, *Possession*, *Gozu*, etc.

Academy Awards, Oscars. The glitzy, glamorous award ceremony that takes place annually in Hollywood, where filmmakers, actors, and other members of the showbiz elite gather to celebrate their achievements. Millions of people tune in to see who will win, who's wearing what, and which celebrated actor will assault a comedian on stage, before coming back to stage to pick up his award. It's awesome!

Academy Leader. The stress-inducing prelude to a movie that gives the projectionist just enough time to scramble and get the projector started before the film starts. A crucial component for keeping audiences from staring at a blank screen for an awkward amount of time.

Academy of Motion Picture Arts and Sciences, AMPAS, The Academy. The Hollywood trade organization, dedicated to the advancement of motion pictures, overseen by representatives from each branch of the film industry. Where film elites get to pat each other on the back and pretend like they're saving the world one award show at a time.

Academy Ratio. The standard aspect ratio used in the film industry from the late 1920s to the early 1950s. It's a staple of old movies, Wes Anderson movies, and whenever modern filmmakers want to evoke a sense of nostalgia for the classic era of cinema.

Accent Light. A type of lighting used in cinematography to highlight or draw attention to a specific subject or object in a scene. Typically placed behind or to the side of the subject to create a rim of light around its edges, separating it from the background and making it stand out.

Accountant. The financial wizard responsible for managing the film's finances. They're the ones making sure your checks don't bounce!

ACE, American Cinema Editors. An honorary society of film editors who are voted into membership on the basis of their professional achievements and shared hatred for Michael Bay movies.

Acetone. A natural chemical used to produce film cements, clean film splicing equipment, and remove nail polish. It smells horrible and is highly flammable, so keep it away from people, pets, and Pyromaniacs.

Acquisitions, Acquisition Executive. A studio executive responsible for buying the distribution rights to finished films or films in the process of being made. They're the folks you *want* sitting at the front row of a festival screening!

Act. A distinct segment that breaks the story into specific parts. A traditional story structure often includes three acts: the beginning (Act I), middle (Act II), and end (Act III). Act I sets the stage, introduces characters, and presents the main conflict. Act II is usually the longest, developing the conflict, character arcs, and introducing plot twists. Act III resolves the conflict and concludes the story. While the three-act structure is common, some narratives may use different act numbers for more complex storytelling, such as Shakespearean plays which typically follow a five-act structure.

Acting Coach. A mentor, a friend, a therapist, and drill sergeant all in one; helps actors bring their A-game to set and fuel the director's drinking problem.

Action Camera, POV Camera. A tiny but mighty digital camera designed for capturing all the thrills, spills, and heart-stopping action from a character's POV. Examples include GoPro, Polaroid Cube, and the DJI Action 2 Power Combo.

Action Cut. An edit that uses on-screen motion, or action, to cover the transition, making the action appear continuous and uninterrupted.

Action Film. A popular movie genre containing action sequences, blowing stuff up, shooting stuff, stunts, Keanu Reeves, Charlize Theron, and Tom Cruise. Some successful examples include the *John Wick* series, *The Matrix*, *James Bond*, *Atomic Blonde*, and *Top Gun*.

Action Safe Area. The section of the screen area where elements are guaranteed to be visible when displayed on a TV or monitor. Word to the wise: keep the important stuff within the box.

Action! Means "go!" The word called, whispered, yelled, or screamed by a film director at the start of each take.

Actor. A person who plays a character on screen. There's no film without them, unless... It's a documentary.

Adaptation. A film or TV show that has been adapted from a written work, often from a novel or a play but also from a comic book/strip, poem or animated cartoon.

Additional Camera, B Camera. An extra camera rented by the production to capture additional coverage from different angles and to film secondary scenes and inserts; it can save *your* life, but make your boom op's miserable.

Adjusted Gross Deal, Gross Deal. A film distribution deal wherein the producers receive an advance (upfront payment) in addition to a portion of the film's net profits (if there are any!). It's like getting paid for your movie twice, once for making it, and once for selling it. What a concept!

Adlib. An improvised line of dialogue, uttered at the director's delight and at the writer's disgust.

Adobe After Effects. A digital motion graphics, VFX, and compositing software popular among indie filmmakers for producing low-cost (yet impressive!) visual effects and titles. In short, it's an awesome little tool that can do pretty much anything.

Adobe Premiere. A timeline-based video editing application released by Adobe to compete with Avid and Apple's Final Cut Pro. It's known for "attempting to save your current project" while you experience chest pains on the editing room floor.

Adobe RGB. A digital color space containing a wider range of color than the popular sRGB color space. RGB stands for "Red, Blue, Green."

Adobe Systems. A software company creating multimedia applications such as the Adobe Creative Suite. Their apps include After Effects, Premiere, Audition and Photoshop, amongst others.

ADR, Automated Dialogue Replacement. The painstaking process of re-recording lines of dialogue in a recording studio and synching it with the actor's lips as if it had been recorded on location. Most often used to replace lines of dialogue captured over loud generators or whispered by actors 20 feet away from the boom.

ADR Editing. The process of editing, matching and mixing ADR sound.

Advance Screener. A physical or digital copy of a film sent in advance of its release to a lucky few who get to see it before everyone else, who then inevitably pirate it and distribute it online for the rest of the world to see. Not cool!

Advance. An upfront payment paid by a film distributor to an over-enthused filmmaker for the purpose of securing a film's distribution rights. It's your dream, and you're going to make it happen damnit!

Aerial, Aerial Shot. A bird's eye view of the world captured from flying machines like planes, helicopters, drones, and cranes. Or if you're rich enough, a winged pegasus.

Agent. A "person" responsible for negotiating and securing contracts on behalf of talent (actors, directors, etc.) in return for a fee (typically, 10%) and a portion of your soul.

AI, Artificial Intelligence. A computer system specifically designed to carry out tasks usually requiring human intelligence. AI has been increasingly employed within the filmmaking industry, for diverse purposes. Some applications of AI, like planning a film's release schedule or assisting in audio synchronization, are generally accepted. However, when AI encroaches on artistic realms – such as writing, directing, and acting – it becomes a contentious issue. This has been a significant contributing factor to the strikes staged by the Writers Guild of America (WGA) and the Screen Actors Guild (SAG) in Hollywood during 2023. The application of AI in the artistic sector remains a hotly debated topic within the industry.

Air. Compressed, canned air. Often used on a film set to remove dust, debris, and other small particles from delicate equipment and hard-to-reach areas such as camera lenses, sensor filters, audio equipment, and other sensitive electronics. Also, you breathe it.

AKS. Abbreviation for "All kinds of stuff."

Alan Smithee. The sole pseudonym that the Directors Guild of America (DGA) allows directors to use when they hate their movie so much that they want nothing to do with it and wish to remove their names from the credits. Famous examples include *Hellraiser: Bloodline* (Kevin Yagher), *Catchfire* (Dennis Hopper), and *Dune* (David Lynch). So when you see an Alan Smithee credit, the director is basically asking you to consider watching something else.

Allen / Allen Wrench. A nifty little tool that looks like an L-shaped screwdriver, and is essential in fixing stuff.

Alpha channel. The transparent part of an image, allowing VFX artists to literally "delete" objects in the frame. If it's white, you can see it, if it's black, it's gone. Often used to make green or blue backgrounds disappear in post-production and VFX.

Alternate ending. The originally planned ending for a film, replaced with the one used upon the film's release. Sometimes, the alternate ending is better (*Get Out*), sometimes it's worse (*Titanic*), and sometimes it's downright confusing (*Pride & Prejudice*). Sometimes filmmakers shoot two alternative endings because they can't decide yet which ending they like the most.

Ambiance Sound. The naturally occurring sounds generated by the environment of a space or a location, (e.g,. birds in the forest, traffic in the city, etc.).

Ambient Light, Available Light. The main source of light in a scene, sometimes a fixture or natural light that sets the mood.

Amnesiac. A derogatory term for an actor who habitually forgets their lines. They may forget the scene, the lines, their mark, or their own name, but never lunch!

Anachronism, Film Flubs, Goofs. A production element, boom mic, artifact, or Starbucks cup captured on film by mistake and noticed only when the project is released.

Analog / Digital Signal. Analog and digital signals represent two distinct methods of processing and storing information. An analog signal is physical (think audio recorded on a physical tape), while a digital signal is, well, digital (an MP3 or WAV file).

Analog Recording. The art of capturing sound or video through old-school analog signals.

Analog Video. An old-school video signal transferred by an analog signal (S-video).

Anamorphic Format. The technique of capturing widescreen footage by use of an Anamorphic lens.

Anamorphic Lens. A specialized lens that affects the way an image is projected onto the camera sensor. The lens 'squeezes' the image, which is then 'de-squeezed' during post-production to create a stunning, cinematic image that gives your movie look more expensive than it actually is. Anamorphics create beautiful bokehs and provide a unique visual aesthetic that screams "Cinema!!'

Anamorphic Lens Adapters. A cheaper alternative to Anamorphic lenses. They compress images captured by non-anamorphic lenses to produce a similar effect. While they can't produce the same bokeh effect, they do introduce a unique aesthetic and are undoubtedly a superior alternative to the sad reality known as "letterboxing."

Ancillary Rights, Secondary Rights. A clause in distribution contracts which gives filmmakers a percentage of the profits derived from merchandising and other non-distribution or film rental revenue. Such rights include TV spin-offs, remakes, stage adaptations, publishing deals, toys, theme park rides, sexy action figures, soundtrack sales, and products that may get recalled due to lead paint or exposure to toxic plastic.

Angel. A coveted private investor who bestows upon you the funds to make your movie. Because that zombie kitten movie of yours isn't going to fund itself!

Angle of View. The field of view covered by a lens, determined by the focal length of your lens, measured in degrees like a slice of pie. The bigger the slice, the more you'll be able to see in your frame.

Angle. The camera's position in relation to your subject. Examples include: a bird's eye view, a canted angle, or a low-angle shot. It's the direction from which the filmmaker wants to tell the story.

Animation. The illusion of motion, created by manipulating individual frames of still images, drawings, or 3D motion and playing them back at speed to make it look like that mouse is actually chasing after that cat with a sledge hammer.

Anime. A style of film, comic, or episodic animation that is rooted in manga, or Japanese comics. Famous examples include *Spirited Away*, *The Girl Who Leapt Through Time*, and the original 1996 version of *Ghost In The Shell*.

Answer Print, First Trial Print. The first "ready-to-see" film print produced by a lab. Once approved, the Answer Print is sent to duplication and distribution, ready to make your dream come true and prove your sister in law wrong!

Antagonist. The enemy of the protagonist, the bad guy (or "thing") who's preventing the hero from achieving their goal. They might not be the biggest threat in the world, but they're certainly trying their best.

Anthology Film, Anthology. A feature film composed of several vignettes, episodes or short films. Examples include *The Red Violin*, *Four Rooms*, *Invitation to the Dance*, and *Sin City*.

Anti-climax. A lame ending to a thrilling series of narrative beats within a plot where all expectation and rising action ends with a "seriously? That was lame!" In other words, Shyamalan's *The Village*.

Anti-hero. A central character who lacks conventional heroic qualities. Examples include Eric Draven in *The Crow*, Mickey & Mallory Knox in *Natural Born Killers*, and Severus Snape in *Harry Potter*.

Aperture, F-Stop. A measurement of the width of a camera lens opening that regulates the amount of light passing through and reaching the sensor. The lower the F-Stop, the more light can enter through the lens, and the brighter the image can get. "Faster" lenses have lower F-stops, and are capable of producing brighter images. How much light you let into the sensor is dictated by how "wide" the opening is. Wide open aperture (fast / lower F-stop) means a brighter image, closed aperture (slow / bigger F-stop) means a darker image. Wide open aperture (let's say F1.2) means a nice bokeh and a shallower depth of field, while a more closed aperture (let's say F4.8) means that everything is pretty much in focus and your 1st AC can take a break. Easy, right?

Aperture, T-Stop. The mathematical equivalent of an F-Stop, it's a more accurate way of calculating the amount of light passing through the lens, for all the cinema nerd-types out there. To summarize, shooting a screaming actor on an aperture of T3.8 means a darker image, more on-set light is needed to compensate, but everything is in focus; while shooting the same screaming actor on an aperture of T1.2 means a bright image, less light on set needed, and your 1st AC's heart rate is through the roof as they attempt to keep the actor's face in focus!

Apple Box. Sturdy, solid, multipurpose wooden box used by short actors and burly grips for various purposes around a movie set.

Apprentice Editor. Assists the Assistant Editor (it's an entry-level position.) They make a mean cup of coffee and handle everything the Assistant Editor doesn't feel like doing, within legal limits, of course!

APS-C. The size of the digital sensors used in DSLR cameras. Equivalent in size to the Super 35 motion picture film format, something DSLR shooters say to make it sound like their Canon T5i is the bees knees.

Aputure. The company behind some of the coolest and most innovative cinema lighting fixtures, accessories, and software around. I'm not getting paid to say this, I'm just a fan!

Arc Light. Old-school bright light source that used carbon electrodes to illuminate streets and large areas in the film industry during the 19th and early 20th centuries. It was eventually replaced by LEDs.

Arc Shot. A Bayham staple. A shot in which the camera rotates around the actor in a circular motion. See, Bayham.

Arm, Grip Arm. (1) A hefty rod attached to a C-Stand; (2) The sexy, muscular arm of a grip, a common sight on film sets everywhere.

Armoror, Weapon Master. The film set's resident weapons expert and safety guru. Responsible for all weapons (guns, swords, pens, etc.) on and off set and props related to said weapons for the duration of the shoot. Supervises their use and provides instruction for the Actors about how to use them properly and safely at the start of each day.

Arri. The Rolls Royce of film camera manufacturers, this little brand packs a powerful cinematic punch and is responsible for a big chunk of feature films made in Hollywood today.

Art Department. The key department in charge of the visual world of the film. Often under the supervision of the film's Production Designer, this department includes the Art Director, Set Designers, Set Decorators, Construction Coordinator, etc.

Art Director. The person responsible for the design, look, and feel of the film's sets and locations. Reporting to the Production Designer, the Art Director designs sets, as well as oversees graphic design and font usage.

Arthouse Film. A film genre encompassing niche film that is not intended to appeal to general audiences, typically because the film prioritizes artistic expression or experimental themes. Expect unconventional storytelling, bold visuals, and a whole lot of art. Famous examples include *The House that Jack Built*, *High and Low*, *Nymphomaniac*, and *The Tree of Life*.

Artifact, Visual Artifact. A pesky little flaw that can ruin an otherwise perfect shot; typically caused by a technical error or equipment malfunction or from the digital, processing or shooting environment. If you're adding them in post for effect, keep artifacts in moderation, less is more!

ASA. An acronym for the American Standards Association, established by Kodak in the 1940s to set up a standard scale for film speeds.

ASC, American Society of Cinematographers. An educational, cultural, and professional organization founded with the purpose of advancing the art and science of cinematography. It's an exclusive club, but hey - never say never!

ASCAP. The acronym for The American Society of Composers, Authors and Publishers. ASCAP is an essential part of these industries in that it tracks the use of copyrighted material so that royalties can be paid fairly to starving artists and satiated copyright owners alike.

Aside. When characters decide to take a break from their fictional world and chat with the audience (or with each other), giving us and their fellow characters a glimpse into their thoughts.

It's what Ferris Bueller and Wayne Campbell do so well!

Aspect Ratio. The proportion of the picture width to height. For example, a perfect square image has an aspect ratio of 1:1. Think of it as the size of the canvas, stretched to fit a cinema screen.

Asperity Noise, Hiss. That annoying background noise that makes you want to throw your headphones across the room. Analog hiss is caused by the inherent noise present in analog recording systems, such as magnetic tape. Digital hiss, on the other hand, is caused by the noise present in digital audio recordings and is generated during the process of converting analog to digital. It's science!

Aspheric lens. A lens whose complex surface can correct or reduce the optical aberrations found in simpler lens designs. It produces better overall quality than spherical lenses, and sharper edge definition. In other words, this shoot is going to cost more than you originally thought it would!

Assembly Cut. The first draft in the editing process where the editor organizes the shots in a particular sequence, meanwhile the director (lamenting on the couch) reevaluates his/her life's purpose.

Assignment By Way of Security. Securing film financing by granting temporary copyrights to the financier as a way of guaranteeing loan repayments. No better way to increase anxiety than to give your dream away to a banker before the first take is in the can.

Assimilate Scratch. A color grading and finishing software, giving your footage that polished look it deserves.

Assistant Art Director (1st, 2nd, 3rd). The art department's right-hand (and left one too); executing the Art Director's vision by helping bring the sets to life.

Assistant Camera, 1st AC. The assistant to the main camera operator. They keep the cameras rolling and make sure the shots are steady and in focus, they like to travel, go for long walks on the beach, and flirt with makeup artists and hot grips in between takes.

Assistant Director, AD, 1st AD. The director's right-hand, the AD sets the shooting schedule, tracks daily progress, arranges logistics, prepares call sheets and maintains organization and order on the set. They also serve as the liaison between the director and the crew, and actors. Recognizable on set by their massive production binders and trademark anxiety.

Assistant Editor. The helpful sidekick to the chief editor, responsible for managing the media files for the project, organizing and labeling footage, sound effects, music, and other media assets, creating rough cuts and assembling scenes, supporting the work of the editor, and ensuring that the project is completed efficiently and effectively as well as boss around interns and pretending to laugh at the editor's strange sense of humor.

Assistant Location Manager. Works as an assistant to the Location Manager. Responsible for distributing pamphlets informing local residents about loud gun-shot sequences and explosions; liaison between crew and location owners. Would also have the fun task of informing the AirBnb host of all the damage caused to their fancy jacuzzi.

Assistant Production Manager. Problem solvers supreme! Assistant to the Unit Production Manager (UPM).

Associate Producer, AP. Works ambiguously under the supervision of the film's producer. They help put the film together in pre-production and keep the ship afloat by any means necessary, to post-production and beyond!

Asynchronous Sound. A mismatched audio track which has not yet been properly synchronized with the image. Someone is going to get yelled at.

ATL Cars. Production cars used by Above the Line personnel. After all, VIP's need to be driven around in style, ATL cars get the job done.

ATL. Abbreviation for Above the Line. Where the big shots reside.

Atmo Cars, Atmosphere Cars. Extra cars and background cars which appear on screen but are not used by the characters in the film.

Atmosphere. Another word for weather or special effects such as smoke, haze, fog, steam, etc. Just make sure it's on in every take, otherwise you'll be crying in post trying to match it.

ATSC Standard. An American set of broadcast standards developed to include both HD and SD formats, irrelevant to most of us, applicable to some of us - that's what this book is all about! #Knowledge

Audience. (1) The group of people who sit in a dark room with strangers and eat overpriced popcorn while watching Hollywood millionaires pretend to be other people on screen. (2) In marketing and distribution terms, the audience is categorized as the potential ticket buyers for a film so that a marketing strategy can be devised.

Audio Bridge. Audio that crosses over from one shot to another, which eases the transition and connects the two shots together. It's like the glue that holds the movie together, making jump cuts less noticeable.

Audio. In short? Sound. It's sound.

Adobe Audition. A digital audio workstation from Adobe Systems that allows you to tweak, adjust, and mix your audio - making your film sound awesome.

Audition. A test performance given by an actor to demonstrate their ability to play a character in the film. Most often performed in a studio or rehearsal space, NOT in a creepy old man's hotel room!

Auteur. Auteur filmmakers have a distinctive approach to filmmaking and their control over the film is so unbounded and personal that the director is likened to the "author" of the film. Examples include Quentin Tarantino, Wes Anderson, Christopher Nolan, and you. Yes, you didn't expect me to build your confidence up, did you? Aim high and think big, that's the underlying theme of this book.

Auto Conform. The automated process of producing a time-coded EDL file (Edit Decision List) from an offline editing system to replace proxies with broadcast-quality files.

Autodesk. The company that makes your 3D dreams come true with software programs like 3DS-MAX, Maya, Flame, and Smoke.

Autodesk Flame. A premium 3D VFX. finishing and color grading software.

Autodesk Maya. A 3D animation software used in feature films and CG animations to create various VFX, from producing explosions to stormy oceans, to 3D-modeling spaceships and erotic clowns - it does it all!

Autofocus. The camera function that lets you sit back and relax, leaving the focus pulling to technology! It was once viewed as the Antichrist among cinematographers, but with technology improvements, it's gradually becoming a thing of the future.

Automated Dialogue Replacement, ADR. See, ADR.

Available Light. Any light source which is naturally available. For example, the sun. So no need to bring in a big ol' lighting kit, just let nature do the work!

Average Metering. The camera's way of saying "I got this!" It combines all the light values to create the perfect exposure, leaving you more time to perfect your coffee-to-camera-operating ratio.

AVID. Manufacturer of the popular non-linear editing system, Avid Media Composer. When people say "for Avid", they typically mean "for the editing room."

AWB, Auto White Balance. In-camera function that automatically adjusts the scene's color balance to a neutral color regardless of lighting conditions. Your DP will hate it, and you, if you mention it.

Axis of Action. Another term for the 180 rule, because sometimes it's just easier to call it something else. The 180 Rule is a filmmaking guideline for the camera's position in a dialogue scene where the characters are facing each other. In a nutshell, characters should always have the same left to right relationship with each other. If Actor A is facing right, then Actor B should be facing left. If we have to explain the 180 rule one more time… (famous last words)

B

B-Movie. A low budget eye fest; typically the cheaper, second-fiddle film in a double-feature, with enough monsters, horror, crime, and cheesy one-liners to keep you entertained for 90 minutes or so. Examples include *The Giant Claw*, *X: The Man with the X-Ray Eyes*, *Mac and Me*, and *Machete*.

Babies, Baby Sticks, Baby Legs. Tiny tripods, perfect for getting those low-angle shots that make your footage look like it was filmed by a toddler. Also, cute little creatures that almost everybody loves.

Baby Mount. A little guy with a big personality, the mount allows grip gear and lighting equipment to be affixed to stuff via a 5/8" pin or hole.

Baby Plate. A metal plate designed to mount baby-mount fixtures to walls, floors, and apple boxes.

Back End or Back End Points. A term used in contract negotiation to address "profit participation" - meaning that should a film break-even; the eligible (and very lucky) producer may receive some portion of the film's profits.

Back In. The battle cry of a perturbed AD, announcing that lunch is *finally* over and it's time to get back to making movies.

Back lot. An open space beyond "the studio lot" itself, used to construct open sets for filming nature or outdoor scenes. It's where horse-riding cowboys shoot at trains and eat s'mores by the campfire before making passionate love to each other in a tent - in other words, where dreams come true, outside!

Back Projection, Rear Projection. A technique whereby live action is filmed in front of a screen projecting the background action. Most often used in car driving scenes and low-budget B movies.

Back to One. A colloquial phrase to inform the cast and crew to resume their starting positions when it is decided that another take is needed; often due to technical errors or an actor forgetting their lines.

Backdrop. A large piece of cloth hung across the rear of a stage or behind a window to serve as a scenic background. It's cheap and it sells! So long as it isn't windy.

Background Artist, Matte Artist. An artist responsible for painting and designing backgrounds either manually or digitally (matte paintings). Most often in fantasy or Sci-Fi films.

Background Music. Music used to establish the atmosphere and mood in a scene.

Backing. Every filmmaker's dream (or nightmare!) The term is used to define a film that is backed by a movie studio. Getting studio backing typically means you get to make *your* movie the way *the studio* wants you to make it. But on the bright side, you get all the drugs and attention that money can buy - so there's that.

Backlight. A light mounted behind a subject for the purpose of illuminating their back, hair and shoulders, "separating them" from the backdrop to create the illusion of depth. It's a crucial part of the three point lighting setup (Key, Back, Fill).

Backstory. A character's past life, like a secret diary that holds the key to understanding their behavior and actions in the story.

Balance. A term used to define the composition and the aesthetic quality of a film, a scene, soundtrack, color or light. Saying that a shot looks balanced sounds ambiguous, but cool - so feel free to say it as often as you can.

Balloon Light, Helium Daylight Balloon, Self-Illuminated Balloon. A floating light source used to provide a soft and diffused light for those tricky night scenes. They can be tethered to the ground or suspended in the air like a hot air balloon ride at a carnival.

Banana. A direction given to an actor by the director when blocking the scene. Specifically, that the actor must walk in an arc (or a banana shape) when moving toward or away from the camera so that the action will look natural and not stilted. Funny how much unnatural stuff goes into looking more "natural" on film.

Banned Film. A movie prohibited from release due to political, moral, religious, or social reasons. The reasons are often dumb (*Wonder Woman* was banned in the Middle East because it made an Israeli Jew look good), often funny (*The Simpsons Movie* was banned in Myanmar because of the excessive use of the colors yellow and red, which is prohibited in the country), and sometimes plain dumb (Sweden temporarily banned *E.T.* because it portrayed adults as the "enemies of children.").

Bar sheets, Exposure sheets. The blueprint for an animated film's dialogue, listing the number of frames needed for each shot like a super-creative "to do" list.

Barn doors. Folding black metal doors mounted on all four sides of a light source, used to control the direction of the light.

Barney, Sound blanket. A sound-suppressing blanket placed over loud objects on set, such as booming film cameras, air conditioners, computer fans, and fish tanks. Can also be used as a comfy blanket for those rainy days when you just want to stay in and cuddle with a dirty apple box.

Barrel Distortion. An optical distortion common in some wide-angle lenses and zoom lenses that cause the images to be distorted.

Based on a True Story. A film narrative that has some basis in real historical events, proving that truth is stranger than fiction. Famous examples include *The Aviator*, *127 Hours*, *The Fighter*, and *The Wolf of Wall Street*.

Bayham. The over-the-top, explosion-packed filmmaking style of Michael Bay. The term "bayham" refers to blowing stuff up on a massive scale, in slow motion, while the camera pans around the action in low angle. It's awesome!

Bazooka. A grip arm that connects the camera to a dolly for a smooth and sturdy ride. Not to be confused with that thing you use to blast unsuspecting jeeps in Grand Theft Auto.

BCU, Big close-up, ECU. A very close close-up shot in which the subject occupies most of the frame. It's beautiful, emotive, and calls attention to itself, so use it wisely.

Beat. (1) A purposeful moment during a scene, with or without dialogue, that usually entails a significant pause or emotional shift within the character due to circumstance or information given; (2) A plot point in a screenplay that affects the action of the story. (3) That thing your heart skips when Ryan Gosling and Emma Stone share a kiss on screen.

Beaver Board. An apple box with a baby plate screwed into it. Not the lovable furry thing you thought it was.

Bed. Background music used with narration. Also, you sleep on it.

Beefy Baby. While it sounds like a baby that goes to the gym, it's not. It's actually a Matthews stand that can handle tricky terrain, even if it's on stairs or uneven surfaces.

Beep. See, 2-pop. Or don't, I don't care.

Behind the Scenes, BTS. A glimpse into the world of making movies; like watching how your favorite food gets made.

Below the Line, BTL. The physical production costs not included in the Above the Line section of the budget. In general, BTL costs tend to be the costs associated with the actual physical production of the film. For example, equipment rentals, transportation, craftsmen, crew wages, set design, accountants, and post-production workers are all paid from the below the line budget.

Below the Title. Credits for all the non-big-shots on set, appearing at the end of a movie; it's the opposite of Above the Title.

Best Boy Grips (Light, Grip, Electric). The chief assistants to their department heads - the Gaffer and Key Grip. Best Boy Grips act as department foremen (and women!), responsible for the day-to-day operations of the light and grip departments. Feed them well and stay on their good side!

Best light. A color correction term used to refer to a single grade performed in one pass with one color correction setting that applies to the whole sequence, as opposed to an individual shot-by-shot color correction. "Yeah, I'm not color grading this whole thing", is what we tell ourselves as we select/right-click on all the shots to match them. #Magic

Beta. Short for Betamax video tapes, your great grandfather's streaming service.

Betacam. An analog component video format using Beta tapes for SD broadcasting; it's old, grainy, and awesome!

Billing. A talent's credit placement, whether that be in a film's opening credits, closing credits, publicity materials, and/or theater marquee. You know that film you pitched to Jim Carrey? Be sure he'll ask for top billing. His assistant however, can get billed below the title - people go to war over this stuff!

Bin. In film editing, a bin is the storage container used to organize motion picture film and sound stock. In the digital age, it is commonly referred to as the virtual "bin" in which editors store clips for use in a sequence.

Binder Clip. Often used by a cinematographer as a cheap alternative for Grip Clips. When it comes to money, saving is caring!

Biopic. A biographical film that dramatizes the life of a famous (or just plain interesting) person. Famous examples include *Capote*, *The Elephant Man*, *The Social Network*, *Oppenheimer*, and *Lincoln*.

Bird's Eye View. A type of overhead shot in which the camera presents a scene from the point of view of a bird, a plane, or, you know... Superman.

Bit part, Under Five. A minor acting role with few lines of acting, literally meaning under five lines. A famous example is Estelle Reiner's line, "I'll have what she's having" in 1989's *When Harry Met Sally*, or "I don't think so, Jack!" in my yet-to-be-optioned screenplay, *Heroine Chipmunk*.

Bit. The smallest possible unit of digital information. Digital images are often described by the number of bits used to represent each pixel. It's that thing you refer to when you complain about your Sony A7s II.

Biz. A douchey term used in reference to "the business", "movie business", or "show business." Typically by dudes in suits who wear sunglasses at night.

Black and White, B&W. A film with no other colors except for black, white, and shades of gray. Prior to the invention of color film stock, all films were shot in black and white. Nowadays, black and white is an artistic choice, because, you know... cinema!

Black Comedy, Dark Comedy. A humorous film that finds humor in an otherwise sad or dark subject matter. Famous examples include *Fargo, Ready or Not), Death to Smoochy,* and *Plucked* (in theaters 2024) #ShamelessPlug

Black Crushing. A color correction technique that makes shadows darker and less detailed, like in Noir films or especially dark scenes. It's that thing where your DP spent hours on set perfecting, only for you to later "make it darker" in post. Whoops.

Black Level Signal. In post-production, the black level signal refers to the level of darkness in the image. It is the lowest level of brightness that can be displayed in the image without any detail being lost in the shadows. By adjusting the black level signal, colorists can create a more balanced and visually appealing image, enhancing the overall look and feel of the film.

Black Wrap. The knight in shining armor on set; a black foil that saves the princess in distress (the shot) by wrapping light sources, preventing any light spillage, making her look her most beautiful. #Metaphors

Blacklisting. A dark chapter in Hollywood history, where writers, directors, and actors were shunned and banned from the industry, often for false or unproven allegations of allegiance to the Communist Party during the '40s, '50s and '60s. As depicted in the 2015 biopic, *Trumbo*.

Blackmagic. A series of cinema cameras and other equipment by the Blackmagic Design company.

Blackmagic Davinci Resolve. An all-in-one film editing and color grading suite; famous for how awesome it is. (This book was brought to you by Davinci Resolve!)

Blaxploitation. A funky film genre that emerged in the '70s and is considered to be a subgenre of exploitation film. Examples include: *Shaft*, *Blackenstein*, *Foxy Brown*, *Across 110th Street*, and *The Human Tornado*.

Bleach Bypass, Skip Bleach, Silver Retention. A color effect created when the bleaching step in color film development is skipped, either on purpose or just because the "lab dude" forgot to do it (that's not a thing, is it?). A bleach bypass results in higher contrast, lower saturation, and increased graininess in images. Famously used in movies like *American Gangster*, *City of Lost Children*, and *Alien: Resurrection*.

Blimp. A sound-suppression housing unit for noisy cameras; designed to suppress loud noises, not to be confused with a sound blanket, or a pair of good headphones.

Blip Tone. A sync "pop" sound, used to establish a sync point for editing.

Blockbuster. (1) A commercially-successful, lavishly produced, true "Hollywood" movie, filled to the brim with explosions, fast cars, and beautiful people. Designed to make you forget about the sad realities that awaits you at home, while you watch awesome things on the big screen. (2) The name of a once-great home movie rental company, dethroned by Netflix in 2007.

Blocked Shadows. A term used to describe the lack of shadow detail in an image. Generally, it is the result of underexposure or of a low-resolution imaging sensor. It's like a dark cloud hanging over an inexperienced DP on set. #NoPressure

Blocking, Block Out a Scene. A rehearsal practice in which the director details how, where and when the actors will move in relation to each other and, most importantly, to the camera. Blocking determines the movement of actors and the camera in a scene, as well as the consequent placement of lights, grip, and gear. You can't call "action" without it!

Blonde, Mighty. (1) An open face 2K lighting unit; (2) a really cool dream I had.

Blood Capsules. Fake blood pills hidden in the actor's mouth that simulate bleeding. A must-have tool for any SFX makeup artist. They're a fun Halloween trick and a low budget horror film staple, just don't swallow too much of that stuff, it'll mess you up!

Bloop. A distinct sound produced by an audio system when a film splice passes the photocell to which an amplifier is connected.

Blooper. A humorous mistake by a cast or crew member caught on camera. Bloopers offer a look into the way hilarious mistakes on set can diffuse a week's worth of tension and get even the most hardened gaffer or grip to giggle like a 5-year-old.

Blooping Tape. A small opaque tape used to silence undesired portions of sound tracks, generally caused due to a passage of the splice through a sound reproducer. The process is referred to as Blooping. Old tech is awesome, ain't it?

Blow-Down. The opposite of a blow-up. Also, something sexually inappropriate, I'm sure.

Blow-Up. (1) The process of enlarging a film frame to a larger gauge, e.g., 16mm to 35mm or 35mm to 70mm. (2) Something you do to a car or a helicopter (hopefully) on-screen.

Blowout. The complete loss of highlight detail in an image, generally caused due to overexposure.

Blue-screen. The opposite of green-screen, used primarily for dark scenes. So if you want your shots to look like they're being filmed on a sunny beach in Hawaii, go green. But if you're looking to create a moody and mysterious atmosphere, blue is your friend!

Blurb. A snippet of a film review, used to market, promote, and advertise your movie.

Bobbinet. A type of mesh fabric that is commonly used for creating scrims, backdrops, and draperies.

Body Double, Double. A shy actor's best friend! A Body Double is hired to take the place of an actor in scenes that require an aesthetic close-up, generally of a body-part; most often in nude scenes. Not to be confused with Stunt Double or Stand-In. Body doubles are more often than not, responsible for your excitement at a naked [insert deliciously hot celebrity here].

Body Makeup. Unlike face makeup, body makeup is applied to an actor's body for a variety of effects including: tattoo cover-ups, bloody wounds, prosthetic blending, the list goes on. SFX makeup artists really can do it all!

Bogie. (1) A "person" who ruins the shot by walking in front of the camera unannounced. (2) Any uninvited guest on set, who thinks they're the star of the show.

Bokeh. A term that describes the way a lens renders lights that are out of focus. It's like a blur, but with more beauty, style, flair and flare. The more unique the bokeh, the more excited your DP gets.

Bomb, Box Office Bomb. A financial catastrophe of a movie that fails to sell enough tickets to pay for itself. It's like a car crash, hard to look away.

Bongo Ties. A must-have accessory for keeping equipment, cords, and cables organized. Because a set can't run on disorganization, well it can, but it'll get messy.

Book, to be "off book." Meaning an actor has memorized their lines so well, they could recite them in their sleep, or on screen preferably.

Booking Board. Another term for DOOD. A chart used to calculate the number of paid days for each cast member and crew member prior to creating the film's budget.

Boom Microphone, Boom Mic. A long pole with a microphone attached to its end, used to capture the movie's audio. Its design allows for the boom operator to move about the set and get in your shot in all sorts of interesting ways.

Boom Operator, Boom Op. A crew member whose job is to maneuver the Boom Mic and keep it out of shot(!) while also making sure adequate sound is captured. On low-budget sets, the Sound Mixer may have to double as a boom op... it's a rough life for folks with weak arms.

Boom Pole. A telescoping, counter-balanced pole from which a camera or microphone can be suspended. It really puts the "BOOM" in "Boom Operator". Get it?

Bootleg. An illegally copied and pirated version of a film, once sold in street corners to kids worldwide, now distributed for free on the internet.

Bottom Chop. A flag that helps block light from illuminating the floor and ruining an otherwise perfectly lit shot.

Bounce-Board, Bounce, Bounce Light. A white, silver, or gold foam card used to soften harsh light. The light source is "bounced" off the board to create a softer, more diffused light. A must have in every cinematographer's bag of goodies!

Bowdlerize. To sanitize a film's content, removing all the adult themes and vulgar elements, so it can be sold to a mass market audience or to younger viewers.

Box Rental, Kit Fee, Box Fee. An additional fee paid to a crew member who brings and uses their own equipment on set. It's like getting paid for bringing your own tools to the job site.

Box Office. (1) A term used to describe ticket sales. (2) A term used to define the commercial success or failure of a theatrically released film. The higher the box office, the bigger the gross, and the bigger your chances of making sequels until you and your IP fade into obscurity (or irrelevance.)

Bracketing. The method of shooting the same sequence several times with different camera settings to achieve a certain effect. Works primarily on stills, but can translate to film if you stay perfectly still (or if you can afford a motion control camera system.)

Branch Holder. A pipe-like unit used to hold real tree branches, wooden poles, or other items either in front of the lens or a light source. Used to make fun and interesting foregrounds, shadows, and lawsuits (when one inevitably falls and hits someone on the head).

Break Even. That sweet spot where box office ticket sales are enough to cover the film's cost, and the profits start rolling into the studio's pocket like a never-ending ice cream sundae.

Breakdown Artist (Costume Design). A costume artist specializing in "breaking down" garments; they take brand new clothing and make them look old and worn; like a reverse time machine for wardrobe.

Breakdown. A pre-production Bible, more or less. Each scene of the film is broken down, planned for, and itemized by cast, crew, props, equipment, etc. so that come shoot time, everything and everyone is ready to go.

Breast Line. A guideline attached to items being hauled up on a crane or by a pulley.

Bridging Shot. A shot or effect which indicates the passage of time.

Broad Lighting. A lighting setup where the side of an actor's face that is closer to the camera is lit more brightly. This is the opposite of the more popular Short Lighting, where the same applies to the actor's side that is farther from the camera.

Brute, Maxi Brutes. A massive lighting fixture commonly utilized in television and film productions to illuminate expansive areas. Its powerful output ensures that fewer units are needed to achieve the desired lighting level.

Building a Scene. The editing process of putting together the various shots that compose a scene, ideally creating the makings of a satisfying ending. The editor, much like a master chef, must build, layer by layer, his editorial masterpiece.

Bullet Time, Time Morphing. A visual effect that enhances a slow-motion shot by allowing the camera to move around and through a slow-motion shot at normal speed. The term was trademarked by Warner Bros following the release of *The Matrix*. It's Hollywood CGI magic at its finest!

Bump. (1) In film budgeting, a Bump is an extra payment paid to a stunt-person based on the difficulty and dangerousness of the stunt. It's like a bonus for being crazy brave. (2) A monetary incentive given to a performer based on a specific added task that requires extra effort. Under the terms of their agreements, movie stars can get a festival bump (bonus paid when a movie hits a certain festival), a press bump, and others. In short, it's a bonus for being awesome.

Bumper. The often never-ending segment running before the start of a film that displays the trademarks and logos of all the studios, production companies, and distributors that made the movie happen. Often cool (Bad Robot), sometimes ambiguous (Monkeypaw Productions) and otherwise irreverent (Hot Jam Productions).

Burn Out. (1) A type of overexposure that occurs when a portion of the image is exposed to too much light, causing it to lose detail and become completely white. Can be intentional or accidental and can be used as a creative effect in some cases. (2) When a filmmaker tries to do too much stuff before crawling into a corner in the fetal position, they're burned out!

Burn-in Timecode, BITC. The process of superimposing a timecode over part of the picture. A must-have for all editors sending out edits for review. The timecode references the master sequence timecode of the film's edit, making it easier for the receiving party to once again complain about the shot at "0:23:03."

Bus. An auxiliary audio track used for grouping two or more tracks together for processing. Also, it's that big wheely thing you force your actor to take to set when there's no travel budget.

Butt Splice. A splice made by joining two pieces of motion picture film together when the ends do not overlap.

Buyer. The person in charge of purchasing supplies for their department, examples include: SFX Buyer, Prop Buyer, Wardrobe Buyer, etc. They're like personal shoppers for each department, buying the necessary stuff you need to get your movie made (save your receipts!).

Buzz track. An old school, technical term for "Room Tone", or the sound that just exists in the space that you're shooting in, gear and people included.

Buzz. The "talk" about a film that spreads by word of mouth like wildfire. Not to be confused with Hype, which is usually created by a company or individual with a profit motive; buzz is all about people talking and spreading the word organically. Reputation is everything!

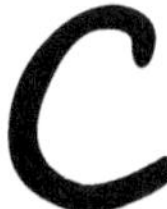

C Stand, Century stand. A nifty, multi-use grip stand, found on nearly every film set. Primarily used to hold silks, flags, or nets in front of light sources, and to unburden sweaty crew members everywhere.

C-Mount. An old-school screw-mounted lens used primarily on 16mm cameras.

C47, Peg. Used for attaching gels and diffusion to barn doors. It's the ultimate clip, holding everything together with a tight grip. #RhymeYourWaytoSuccess

Cable Sync. A cable that is used to synchronize the timing of various pieces of equipment used in the production, such as cameras, sound recording devices, and lighting equipment, allowing them to be triggered simultaneously.

Cableperson, Utility Sound Technician, Sound Assistant. The person responsible for laying, connecting, and concealing cable wires on set. If you trip over a loose wire, it's probably their fault.

Call Sheet. A document issued by the 1st AD to the cast, crew, and production staff (typically sent in the wee hours of the morning), to inform folks of the date, time, and location at which to report for the following day of filming. Contains many nifty details about the day in question, such as the set's proximity to a hospital, weather, and sometimes– inspirational quotes. Said sheet is typically sent in a "thank you for all your hard work" email, because in this game - gratitude is everything!

Call Time, Call. The time to report to set, like a school bell ringing; signals the start of the day.

Cameo. A small role played by a big star, seemingly out of nowhere! Famous examples include: Stephen King in *It: Chapter 2*, David Bowie in *Zoolander*, Matt Damon in *Thor: Ragnarok*, and Bill Murray in *Zombieland*. It's like a surprise party, with a well-known guest showing up for a few minutes.

Camera Accessories. In film budgeting, this line includes anything that doesn't come as part of the camera package: lenses, remote focus pullers, batteries, shoulder rigs, and that extra monitor that no one uses.

Camera Angle. The camera's viewpoint that makes a scene come to life, it's like selecting a seat in the theater, the direction from which the filmmaker wants to tell the story.

Camera Assist, 1st AC, First Assistant Camera. The trusty sidekick to the Camera Operator, helping them keep shots in focus and avoiding blurry nightmares, as well as setting up and maintaining camera equipment, stabilizing gimbals, loading and unloading film (or memory cards).

Camera Blocking. The elaborate dance routine where the camera, cast, and crew all perform their moves in perfect harmony before the cameras start rolling, and the wireless monitor starts acting up.

Camera Crew. The team responsible for the operation of the cameras on set. Job titles include: the Camera Operator, Cinematographer, 1st and 2nd AC, Dolly Grip, etc. They're an awesome group of gearheads who love a good pat on the back, and appreciate a pretty shot when they see it.

Camera Dolly. A specialized wheeled cart installed on a track for the purpose of producing smooth camera movements. It's how you get those nice push-in shots (also known as Dolly Shots) you've always dreamt about.

Camera Loader, Clapper-Loader. The person in charge of operating the clapper and loading ammo (film stock) into film magazines. This job is typically handled by the 2nd AC, or on low budget indies, whomever is standing closest to the camera.

Camera Log, Camera Report. A written, detailed form used to log shots and track details such as lenses, filters, and other camera settings for each shot taken on the day

Camera Monitor. An external monitor on which crew-members can see what the camera is filming without getting in the way and breathing loudly in the operator's ear.

Camera Noise. The audible sound emitted by the camera. Not to be confused with Picture Noise. Both are considered to be "the enemy" by the boom operator, cinematographer, and editor alike.

Camera Operator, Camera Op. The crew member responsible for operating the camera. Make sure they get plenty of coffee, but not too much that their hands begin to shake.

Camera Stock. Another word for film stock.

Camera Tape. A white cloth tape used for many purposes on-set, mainly for labeling magazines. Not to be confused with Gaff Tape.

Camera Wedges. Small wooden wedges used to level cameras on uneven terrain; because when life gives you lemons, you make lemon wedges!

Camera. A device fundamental for capturing images. Movie cameras take a series of still images (or "frames") consecutively; when they are played at a certain speed (hopefully, 24 frames-per-second), the illusion of motion is created. Hence, the motion picture camera. I bet you knew that already, but it's always fun to be reminded!

Can, "In the Can". A term used to suggest that all the shots have been completed, a film or a scene is ready for post, and you and your crew are clear for vodka! The phrase comes from the early days of filmmaking when movies were shot on physical film stock, which was stored in metal film cans.

Candela, Candlepower. A measure of light intensity that's equivalent to the warm glow of a standard candle. While candlepower was commonly used in the past, it has been largely replaced by the unit of measurement called lumens. Lumens provide a more accurate and consistent measurement of the amount of light emitted by a source, and are now the preferred unit of measurement in the film industry.

Candlelight. The warm and cozy lighting provided by candlelight or a small fire. It's soft, pretty, and makes you want to cuddle under a blanket.

Candy Glass, Sugar Glass. Fake glass that won't cut people. Used to to substitute real glass when a human being has to fly through it, because getting hurt on set is not as fun as it looks.

Candy Bag Alts, Candybags. A list of alternative lines of dialogue, written at the last minute, typically in a comedy, which the actor reads without rehearsing. Just in case you wanted to be a screenwriter and feel what it's like to die inside.

Canted Frame, Dutch Angle, Dutch tilt. A camera frame that's angled and rotated to create a sense of uneasiness or tension. It's like a shot that's dizzy and can't keep its balance. Useful for when a character walks in on something they shouldn't have!

Transportation Captain. The chauffeur of the film world who ensures everyone gets to set on time and in style.

Caption, Closed Captions. A descriptive line of text that appears at the bottom of the screen, not to be mistaken for subtitles. Closed captions provide a full transcription of the audio content, while subtitles provide a translation of the spoken dialogue.

Car Rig. A device used to mount a camera or other piece of equipment, onto a car. It beats the alternative of just poking the camera out the window; either way, it makes a really cool sound when you hit a bump and it comes crashing down onto the asphalt.

Card Reader/Writer. A device which transfers data from a camera's memory card to a computer without the need to connect the camera to the computer directly, because extra cables are for suckers!

Carpenter. Crew members who build a variety of wooden structures and sets; they work with their hands, unlike some people we know…

Carpet Shield. A highly resistant tape used to protect equipment and sets from damage. It can save *you* some money in repairs and save the homeowner from hating you for the rest of their life.

Cash Cow. A successful film that, after it has proven profitable over time, continues to generate substantial revenue. Like a milkable unicorn; examples include *Titanic*, *Avatar*, and *The Dark Knight*.

Cash Flow. Another word for profit. The river of riches that flows through and out of a movie's bank account, minus the studio's expenses of course.

Cast. The shining stars who bring the script to life with their performances; they make us laugh, cry, and fall in love. There's no movie without them, so treat them well and hope for the best!

Casting. The process of auditioning, testing, and presenting a selected group of talented actors to the director so that he or she can decide on who will play the various characters in their film; it's the process of materializing dreams!

Casting Call. A shout out to the world that says "Hey actors! Come audition and be famous!" Typically sent out by the Casting Director on Breakdown Services, or by a small-town indie filmmaker on Craigslist looking to make some stars out of underdogs.

Casting Couch. The shady, and now career-ending and prosecutable practice of powerful position holders soliciting sexual favors from aspiring actors in return for a role in a film. Quid Pro Quo at its worst. It's a dark chapter in film history where women had to trade their dignity for a shot at stardom. Thank God that's no longer happening!

Casting Director. The person hired by production to oversee the casting process. They screen auditions, oversee the casting process, and negotiate with agents and managers. They aim to be your champion in the ring when you're busy with your shot list, find one who really gets you and the story you're trying to tell.

Casting Society of America, CSA. A professional organization of recognized and esteemed Casting Directors.

Catchlight. A synonym for eye light; a cinematography trick that makes actors look alive and vibrant on screen. Something to be avoided if that's *not* what you're going for.

Caterer. The culinary genius who feeds the hungry cast and crew with delicious meals, and sometimes... pizza!

Catharsis. The release of emotional tension that happens at the end of a movie or a scene, when all the pent-up feelings explode and we feel relieved. A form of cinematic orgasm, only with less cuddling after.

Cautionary Tale. Referring to a narrative with a didactic or moralistic message, so - watcher be warned!

CC Filters, Color Compensating Filters. Filters used to fine-tune and control the color balance influenced by light in a scene. Like cinematic instagram filters, only no one is writing hateful comments on your profile page while you cry on the toilet.

Celo Screen. A wax-coated wire mesh designed to protect electrical equipment from rain and snow. Keeps your gear dry during those stormy shoots and ensures your footage doesn't turn into a watercolor painting.

Cement Splice. A method of joining film together by using a chemical glue called film cement.

Censorship. The ultimate party pooper. This process decides what parts of a film are too wild for public consumption, and cuts them out! The audience is left with little more than a shell of what could have been.

CGI, Computer Generated Imagery, CGI Animation. The use of computer-generated images, animations, and visual effects in film. CGI is used to create realistic or fantastical environments, characters, and objects that would be difficult or impossible to create with traditional techniques. It's the digital wizardry that brings your wildest imaginations to life. With CGI, anything is possible, and everything is super expensive!

Chain Of Title. A way of verifying proprietary copyright ownership in a film. One of many reasons to copyright your work (!!!) and keep copies of agreements.

Chain Vice Grip. A clamp vice grip with a chain, in case you need to grip stuff. It features a bicycle-type chain that can be wrapped around poles, pipes, or trees, and then tightened securely using a vice grip.

Chammy. A soft, round pad that wraps around the viewfinder cup. It helps keep the operator's eye closer to the viewfinder display and make them look cool (and comfortable) in BTS stills.

Change Pages. Changes made to the script, often last minute, during the course of production. Kubrick style!

Changeover Cue. A small dot mark at the end of a release print reel (at the right-top corner of the frame) that signals to the anxious projectionist the moment at which to switch over to the next reel.

Changing Bag. A black bag used for loading film into magazines. It's like a portable darkroom, perfect for loading film without the need for a sunless dungeon.

Channel, Audio. An audio channel is like a road for audio signals to travel on - it connects the source (like a microphone or an audio player) to the destination (like a speaker or a recording device). It can refer to a single stream of audio, typically representing a single source, such as a voice or an instrument, or multiple streams of audio, such as in a stereo or surround sound setup.

Channel, Image. A component of a digital image that carries specific information related to its color and brightness values. Each pixel is made up of one or more image channels, each of which represents a specific color component of the image. For example, in an RGB (Red-Green-Blue) image, there are three image channels - one for each primary color.

Character Actor. An actor who specializes in playing well-defined, unique, quirky, or eccentric characters. Examples include Peter Stormare, Johnny Depp, Octavia Spencer, Tilda Swinton, and that friend you know who calls him/herself a character actor.

Character study. A film in which the depiction of the main character's personality is more important than the actual plot. Character studies also refer to when literary students, self proclaimed cinephiles, and movie bloggers write in-depth essays about said characters.

Character. A person in a story, performed by an actor. Characters can also be non-human entities with a perceived "soul"; e.g. animals, machines, inanimate objects, and whatever the hell Jar Jar Binks is supposed to be.

Cheater Cut. The introductory footage at the beginning of a sequel that presents the events that took place in previous films.

Check Print. A print made for the purpose of verifying the look and quality of an effect.

Check The Gate. The phrase called out after "Cut!" that's used to verify that the camera and the film are free from any impurities that might affect the quality of the footage. Filmmakers will call it on digital shoots as well, because we saw Quentin Tarantino do it on a YouTube clip once, and we all want to pay homage.

Checkerboard Cutting. A way of removing the visual "flash" of a film splice to make the edit appear seamless.

Chekhov's Gun. The idea that every detail in a story must have a purpose, or it risks becoming an unnecessary, aimless, and distracting element. So next time you think it's cool to show a character playing with a sword, somebody better get stabbed before the film is over!

Chemistry. Referring to how well two actors work together and complement each other on-screen. It's whatever Amber Heard And Jason Momoa didn't have on the set of *Aquaman*.

Chemistry Read. An audition designed to test the "chemistry" between two or more actors whose characters require a certain innate dynamic between them.

Chiaroscuro. The art of using strong contrast between shadows and highlights to produce a bold cinematic composition. A popular look in film noir.

Chick Flick. Films that stereotypically appeal mainly to female audiences (or most dudes when they think no one is looking). Notable examples include *The Notebook*, *Clueless*, *Mean Girls*, and *When Harry Met Sally*.

Chief Rigger. A crew member responsible for assembling the wire, ropes, booms, lifts, and cables on set.

Child Actor. Any young talent under 18 years of age. Child actors are the future of Hollywood, that is unless cynicism and cocaine gets to them first!

Child Wrangler, Baby Wrangler. Their role is to keep any children in the production safe and accounted for.

Chimera. A high-end softbox used to achieve controlled, beautiful, soft light. A "go to" on every "closeup of a beautiful actress" shot.

China Ball, Lantern. A great low-budget tool for casting an omnidirectional, soft, diffused light, that spreads evenly over a large area. Mount it horizontally or hang it overhead on a boom or from the ceiling to add a soft light to your scene.

Choker. An ominous camera framing angle that cuts the actor right below the chin; a classic choice when trying to pay homage to *Once Upon a Time in the West*.

Chopsocky. A disparaging term for old-school martial arts flicks that bring back memories of high kicks, flying punches, and you and your siblings trying to reenact fight sequences in the living room. The films are awesome, the term… not so much.

Choreographer. These movement artists are responsible for creating the slickest fight scenes and the fanciest of footwork in your favorite action movies and musicals.

Choreography. The specific movement based sequences designed, rehearsed, and performed for film and/or stage. Cue "Jazz Hands."

Chroma key. A process of digital compositing in which a specific color in an image is made transparent. Commonly used to remove green screen and blue screen backgrounds.

Chrominance. The range of colors and hues that can be displayed in an image, as distinct from its brightness or luminance component. Chrominance is an important aspect of color theory and color management in digital imaging and video production.

Chyron. Another name for a "Lower Third" graphic.

Cinch Marks. Film scratches and marks caused by winding or dust between film coils. If you're shooting digital, you'll most likely never encounter this term.

Cinema Audio Society, CAS. A non-profit organization formed in 1964 for the purpose of honoring and recognizing outstanding achievements in sound.

Cinema Verité. A realistic documentary-like (but not) filmmaking style pioneered by Jean Rouch (*The Act of Killing, West 47th Street, Project X, Down for Life,* etc.).

Cinemascope. An anamorphic system used for filming and projecting widescreen films in the 1950s. Makes you feel like you're right in the middle of the action!

Cinematic. A moment, scene, or shot in a film that embodies the "essence" of cinema; oftentimes, a visually appealing shot or an especially emotional moment. Harry Styles said it best, when he said, "it *feels* like a real movie."

Cinematographer, DP, Director of Photography. An artist responsible for making decisions related to the film's cinematography and visual style; they oversee the camera department and work closely with the gaffer and crew to establish what lighting is needed where. They're the ones who make the actors look pretty, so y'all better be on their good side so that they'll be sure to capture yours!

Cinematography. The art and techniques of motion picture photography. It encompasses the use of light, color, camera, lens, filters, and film stock to produce a cinematic image for the screen. A delightful dance between light and shadow, color and texture, creating breathtaking images, whether it be for the big screen or for the tiny ones in your pocket.

Cinephile. A film enthusiast or devotee. Someone who has a passion for film, film theory, history, criticism, and their unsolicited opinions on all of it.

Cinerama. The process of projecting a film from three 35mm projectors to produce a breathtaking panoramic view. Used as a cinematic attraction in the 1950s, it was as close to VR as you could get before VR was a thing.

Cinex Strip. Not a movie theater where patrons strip, but rather the process of testing and printing frames at different exposure levels. A stress test of sorts, where only the best shots make the cut.

Clamp Light. An adjustable lighting fixture that "clamps" onto things, go figure.

Clapperboard, Clapper, Slate. A literal clapping board used to cue the synchronization of picture and sound for editing purposes. A typical slate will mark scenes, shots, and takes with a satisfying "clap." Don't come to set without it.

Classification and Ratings Administration, CARA. The division of the MPAA responsible for administering film rating certificates. See, MPAA.

Claymation. The process of animating clay characters. Famous examples include *Coraline*, *Shaun The Sheep*, and *The Nightmare Before Christmas*.

Clean Speech. A perfect take in which the dialogue was performed without an error, much to the satisfaction of everyone on set but the director, who'd like to take it again from the top.

Clearance, Script Clearance. A legal report that breaks down a script to identify potentially problematic legal issues and red flags ahead of production. Better to know ahead of time what needs to go. After all, you might look good in a suit, but you won't look good in a lawsuit.

Click Track. A series of audio cues set to tempo on a prerecorded track used to ensure proper timing and music sync.

Cliffhanger. An intense, dramatic moment with no conclusion that leaves an audience in suspense. Named for the practice of leaving the main character hanging from the edge of a cliff.

Climax. The peak of anxiety or emotional tension in a story; the moment where all of the rising action comes to a head. It is followed by falling action: catharsis, anti-climax, cliffhanger, and/or feelings of annoyance and hatred for the director.

Clip. A snippet of video or audio.

Clipped Whites. The loss of highlight detail resulting from a peak or limit of an electronic signal. You can only go so bright before things get clipped, if that's not a metaphor for life, I don't know what is. (looking at you Icarus.)

Close-up, CU, Tight Shot. A detailed shot which tightly frames a person or an object; getting up and personal!

Closed caption, CC. A textual representation of the dialog, actions, and sounds in a film; it gives hearing-impaired folks, those who speak another language, or those sitting beside a very loud child, a way to keep up with the action.

CMOS. The main technology used in DSLR cameras.

Co-Producer. A producer responsible for various managerial producing functions. They work closely with the film's chief producer and are integral to problem-solving on set. They help assure that each member of the production team has everything they need in order to do their job properly.

Coaxial Cable. A sturdy copper cable used for video signal transmissions.

Coaxial Magazine. A double-chamber film magazine.

Codec. An application used to encode or decode video for playback and recording. Popular formats include H.264, MPEG, AVCHD and PRO-RES, and whatever the hell was in that Quicktime Codec Megapack thing you downloaded.

Cold Brick. A dead walkie-talkie battery. Often the result of someone smoking too much and "forgetting" to plug it in after last night's wrap.

Cold. (1) The safe state of a prop gun, meaning it's not loaded and therefore can be handled comfortably . (2) The polar opposite of "hot", which is a warning from the prop master or armorer that a weapon is ready to fire (blanks, hopefully!). (3) The wintery state of a turned off or dead mic that's not ready to perform, leaving your actors without a voice and you with a lot of work in post.

Collection Agency. The role of the collection agent is to collect and distribute the proceeds of a film to the contractual participants and investors. Examples include Freeway Entertainment, Fintage House, etc. They're like the Robin Hood of the film industry, minus the giving to the poor part.

Collection Agreement. An agreement made between the producer, financing company, and the collection agent. It helps assure that everyone gets paid on time, and eliminates the possibility of anxiety-inducing shenanigans by greedy studios and forgetful EP's.

Color Balance. The adjustment of the varying intensities of colors from a camera to a monitor, so that no color is diminished or dulled disproportionately by the strength of another; used with the aim of achieving a color "balanced" image.

Color Bars, SMPTE Color Bars. A test pattern used to sync the color and brightness settings of a monitor or projector with those of the footage.

Color Calibration, Monitor Calibration. A process of calibrating a monitor to achieve a more accurate representation of colors.

Color Cast. A color cast refers to an overall wash of color, often unintended, that impacts either a portion or the entirety of your shot. This unintended tint is usually due to environmental lighting, a low-quality lens filter, inexperienced cinematography, or a delightful combination of all these factors.

Color Consultant. A Technicolor advisor providing advice and guidance for projects shooting on film.

Color Correction. The process of adjusting and repairing flaws in color balance, contrast and exposure to make footage seem more natural and unprocessed (an oxymoron, ain't it?). This process is generally followed by a more stylized color grade.

Color Depth, Bit Depth. The number of bits used to define the color of a single pixel, determining how vibrant and stunning your images can be.

Color Grading, Color Grade. The crucial process of altering and stylizing the overall visual feel of a shot or scene by adjusting the color to make it more appealing. This is where the magic happens! In a dark, isolated theater room, with a laser pointer and a color wheel.

Color Space. The range of colors that can be captured and displayed by a camera and/or monitor. It is a mathematical model that describes how colors are represented in digital media, based on a set of primary colors, their intensities, and their relationships to each other.

Color Temperature. The temperature of a light source. A lower value means colder (blue) while a higher value means warmer (orange).

Color Timing. Color timing is the colorization of film as it is being developed and produced in the lab. It involves the photo-chemical process of creating colorized prints by a Lab Timer and is irrelevant to the 95% of filmmakers who shoot their stuff on digital. Just press "record", you'll be fine!

Colorist. A color correction and grading artist who uses digital tools like Resolve and SGO Mistika to manipulate the image and improve the aesthetics of a film.

Colorization. The painstaking process of hand coloring black and white frames in a post-production effort to give old classics new life. Famous examples include: *It's a Wonderful Life*, *Casablanca*, *The Big Sleep*, and *King Kong*.

Combo Stand. The heavy-duty workhorse stand of the lighting world, holding up sizable light fixtures like the M18 and ARRI Skypanel with ease.

Comedy. The oldest film genre, designed to tickle your funny bone and make you forget your troubles. Classically, comedy often results in a happy ending, and who doesn't love that?

Comic Relief. The use of a humorous character or situation in an otherwise serious or tense scene/film. Examples include Leo Getz in *Lethal Weapon*, Ruby Rhod in *The Fifth Element*, and Pintel and Ragetti in *Pirates of the Caribbean*.

Coming-of-Age. A genre of film that portrays the struggles and triumphs of growing up.

Command Performance. When an actor's performance is so exciting and compelling that it stands out among the other performances in the film, therefore "commanding" the audience's attention and leaving you spellbound.

Commentary. a candid take on a scene by a commentator; often a filmmaker, actor, or critic, offering insights and analysis as the film plays in real-time.

Compact Flash Card, CF card, C-Fast. A commonly used mass storage flash card in Canon, Arri, Atomos and Blackmagic cinema cameras. Not to be confused with SD Cards or SDHC cards.

Compander. A noise-reduction device designed to improve audio signal and help your sound engineer sleep at night. Companders are also used in some types of audio equipment, such as wireless microphones and telephony systems, to improve the quality and intelligibility of audio transmissions.

Compilation. A sequence of shots or footage from pre-existing content that is edited together for a new purpose. Like a cinematic remix.

Completion Bond, Completion Guarantee. A form of insurance (or safety net) offered by a guarantor to a distributor or a financier which assures the completion and delivery of a feature film by a given date.

Complication. A plot point that complicates a protagonist's arc in a film or scene. It's the last thing the character wants, and everything that a movie plot needs. Conflict is key!

Component Signal. A high-bandwidth analog video signal, transmitted or stored as three separate signals.

Composer. The musical mastermind behind a film's s core, crafting the tunes that bring the story to life. They are responsible for writing and producing the film's musical score. Famous examples include Hans Zimmer, Howard Shore, John Williams, and those guys who keep emailing you out of the blue.

Compositing. In visual effects (VFX), compositing is the process of digitally combining visual elements from different sources into a sequence, or blending 3D footage with live-action footage. This is generally done to produce shots that cannot be filmed in real life, or would otherwise be impractical to create; i.e. when alien ships crash into the White House or when you feel like going for a stroll on the surface of the moon.

Compositor. The VFX artist, who wields specialized software like After Effects, Nuke or Flame with gusto, bringing visual effects to life. With their mastery of compositing, they ensure that the final product is seamlessly believable.

Compression. A method of reducing the size of an otherwise large digital file to free up storage capacity. Because that folder only you know about takes up a lot of space, and we're not going to delete that!

Concept Art. The illustrator, working in tandem with the production designer, art director, and director, creates various visuals to convey how the characters and the "world" of a film should look.

Condenser. A type of in-studio microphone used for capturing delicate vocals and high frequency sound. It's the perfect tool for capturing audio from that mumbling actor that no one can hear.

Conductor, Musical Conductor. The orchestra's maestro, directing the performance during a scoring/recording session and making sure everything sounds just right.

Construction Coordinator, Foreman, Construction Manager. The person in charge of overseeing and coordinating the construction of sets and stages; because that *Fifty Shades of Grey* dungeon set isn't going to build itself.

Contingency. The safety net of the production budget; a predetermined amount of money (generally 10% of the budgeted cost of production) added to cover potential cost overruns. It's a financial cushion, giving the production peace of mind knowing that they have a little extra in case things don't go exactly as planned, which they rarely do.

Continuity Report. A report that keeps tabs on everything that happens in a scene: changes in clothing, actors' blocking and gestures, camera locations, prop positions, etc. It's the key to maintaining continuity, making sure that the action stays consistent and logical.

Continuity. Another word for consistency – whether in terms of the entire film or within specific scenes or sequences. The person responsible for continuity on set is the Script Supervisor, they ensure that audiences never lose the sense that the action is real and logical. Whether it's the clothing, makeup, or the position of a prop, they keep everything consistent so that you don't get depressed in post.

Continuous. The term is used to describe the unbroken flow of action in a film, where the camera glides smoothly from location to location, scene to scene, or shot to shot, without any jarring cuts.

Contract Player. Any actor under contract to a studio. This was common practice in Hollywood until the 1960s, but now applies only to a handful of Hemsworths.

Contractor. Any independent person on-set who is not represented by a union or guild and who provides a single service to the production. Because "on-set plumber" and "guy who keeps raccoons off the crafty table" are not union jobs... yet!

Contrast, Gamma. The visual difference in luminance and color shading that makes an object visually distinct, so as to "pop-out." It's the secret ingredient that transforms a dull shot into a stunning one.

COO. Abbreviation for the COVID-19 Compliance Officer, the guardian angel of safety on set. They make sure everyone is following the rules, so everyone can work and play together during some otherwise crazy times.

Coogan's Law, The California Child Actor's Bill. A law designed to restrict access to the earnings of child actors so that no adult can exploit a child or benefit by compelling a child to work. Wages are thus protected and preserved for when the child becomes a legal adult and needs to pay for rehab.

Cookie, Cuculoris. A flat board with holes of all shapes and sizes, typically placed in front of a light source in order to create unique shadows and patterns across an object, subject, or backdrop. Just don't try to eat it, it's not good for you!

Co-Production Treaty. A partnership between two nations, making it so production companies can join forces for international co-productions. Filmmakers can work with foreign producers or post-production facilities, enjoying all the tax breaks, benefits, and other incentives that come with them. It's a win-win for everyone involved! Plus, you get travel miles!

Copy, Roger That, Roger. A friendly reminder to let you know that the message has been received loud and clear! It's fun to say, and can easily become a part of your day-to-day vernacular, a double edged sword when she says "I love you" and you respond with, "copy."

Copyright Clearance Center. An organization that processes and tracks licensing services for copyrighted materials. Because, the government's got your back!

Copyright Search. A thrilling journey through the vast archives of the US Copyright Office. It's like a treasure hunt, but instead of treasure, you're searching for the right to use someone else's work in your film.

Copyright. The legal armor that protects your brilliant, mind-bending, Oscar-worthy creations. Once you've submitted your completed film, music, or screenplay to the U.S. Copyright Office, you can rest easy knowing that it won't be pirated and distributed online for all to see (it will, but dammit, you'll have a case!).

Core, Film Tube. A trusty cylinder hub that holds your precious film like a mother hen cradling her chicks. It keeps your film safe and sound until it's ready for its big debut at the local theater.

Corman That Shit. The process by which funds are raised for a film project by use of a concept movie poster or an elevator pitch. A practice mastered by "The Pope of Pop Cinema", Roger Corman.

Costume Buyer. The person who gets to take your credit card and go on a shopping spree! They're responsible for buying all the fabric and garments needed for the costumes.

Costume Design. The department that makes sure everyone in your film looks their best. They research, source, and design costumes for all characters, performers, and extras.

Costume Designer. The head honcho of the costume department, responsible for coming up with the look of all the garments in the film. They sketch their designs, work with the Costume Supervisor, and make sure everyone looks fabulous on the big screen.

Costume Fitting. Imagine a chaotic fitting room with a bunch of actors, measuring tapes, and costumes flying everywhere. That's a costume fitting! It's where the actors try on their wardrobe for the film and make sure everything fits like a glove (or a spaceship captain's uniform).

Costume Standby. A person responsible for costume continuity and assisting the cast with their costumes. They are generally present during the shoot for repairs and minor alterations, for co-ordinating with costume staff, and for wrapping folks in ponchos during crafty, because that dress is a rental and we can't afford to get spaghetti sauce all over it!.

Costume Supervisor. The person in charge of executing the Costume Designer's sketches. They hire seamstresses, manage logistics and budget, all while consulting with the designer to ensure that the costumes turn out correctly.

Counter. A gadget that measures the length of the physical roll of film. It's like a cinematic pedometer, keeping track of the footage, so you know exactly how much you've shot and how much film you have left.

Courtroom Drama. A legal battle that (ideally) skips the boring parts. It's a film genre that takes a serious issue and puts it on trial, exploring the characters and the conflict from all angles within the court of law. These films will have you on the edge of your seat, cheering for justice to be served and for that sexy prosecutor to finally get together with her attractive counterpart. Examples include such films as *To Kill a Mockingbird*, *12 Angry Men* , and *A Few Good Men.*

Cover Me. A simple phrase that means, "Hold my beer, I'll be right back." It's when one crew member asks another to fill in for them while they take a quick break.

Cover Set. A "backup plan" for when things go wrong, like a spare tire or an office spouse - If your intended location falls through, you've got a backup one that you can use instead. It's always good to have a plan B, especially in this unpredictable world of filmmaking.

Coverage, Script. A summary, analysis, and critique of a screenplay. The report summarizes the script, comments on its quality and commercial viability, as well as gives it a score. At its best, it's a super handy tool; at its worst, it's useful for convincing wide-eyed screenwriters that their ideas suck and that they have no talent.

Coverage. The additional footage and camera angles captured during filming that are available to the editor during post-production. More coverage means more options in the editing room. Coverage takes time and effort to capture correctly, but can truly save an edit.

Cowboy. A shot framed from just above the knees of the subject upward. Pretentiously referred to as the "American shot" (*plan américain*) by French film critics.

CPL Filters. A piece of glass that can reduce the glare from reflective surfaces (such as glass or water); can be screwed onto a lens or added to a matte box. Not to be confused with ND filters.

Craft Services, Crafty. The craft services department provides the cast and crew with snacks, drinks, and secret stashes of treats to keep them happy and energized throughout filming.

Crane Shot. A top view of a scene, captured by a camera that's mounted on a crane, jib, boom, or drone; they steal a lot of time on set, so better get them fast and get them right!

Creative Consultant. An ambiguous credit given to a person who has assisted with the creative process in some way. Often granted to the best friend who spent hours listening to you drunkenly talk about your film.

Creator. The primary creative force behind a project. Often, this is the person who dreamed up the concept and manifested it on the big screen.

Credits, Billing. The film's long list of shout-outs to all the people and companies that made the movie possible. Just like a hit Tik Tok video wouldn't be complete without its featured artist and people who shared it, a film wouldn't be complete without its credits. Guild contracts determine who gets top billing, or who gets their name written in big, bold letters above the title of the film, and who gets relegated to the credits in small font below the title.

Crew Call. The precise second at which a crew member is expected to arrive on set. When the AD calls "Present?", you better be there with a smile on your face.

Crew, Crewmembers. The awesome people who make the magic happen. They do it all, from setting up lights and handling makeup, to operating the cameras and climbing ladders. They're the backbone of the production, working tirelessly behind the scenes to bring the filmmakers' vision to life. Treat them well, and they'll hate you less by the end of the shoot.

Cribbing. The temporary wooden structure used by the grip to set up the lights and other equipment.

Crisis PR. A publicist hired to repair the damage caused to a celebrity's reputation and/or career as a result of something terrible they did. After all, just because you did something horrible doesn't mean you are a horrible person, at least that's what they get paid to say.

Crisis. The moment in a film when all hell breaks loose; the tension is at its highest, and the audience is on the edge of their seat. It's the climax of the film, leading to the resolution, conclusion, and then you tweeting about how awesome it was.

Critic. (1) The people who write about upcoming films and give their opinions on the entertainment value and artistic merit of the film. Their reviews can make or break a film's release. (2) Your mom's friend, who isn't sure that you were "destined" to succeed in this industry. Maybe look for a career in waste management instead.

Cross Dissolve. A transition fading from one clip to another, it stands in stark contrast to the jarring transition of a jump cut. It's a staple in dramas, romantic scenes, and '90s wedding videos.

Cross-Conversion. The process of converting NTSC (TV standard used in North America) to PAL (standard used in Europe and other parts of the world) and vice versa.

Cross-Cutting. An editing technique that allows the audience to experience two different scenes at the same time. First used in the classic 1903 film, *The Great Train Robbery,* and has since become a staple in the film industry.

Crossfade. (1) A gradual mix transition between two clips. (2) Not the type of haircut you'd typically ask for.

"Crossing!". A "head's-up!" call to a camera operator that you are about to walk in front of their frame and ruin their shot, even though the camera isn't rolling.

Crossover Film. A studio executive's dream, a crossover is a film which combines two or more characters, worlds, and settings from different literary or film sources for the purpose of appealing to a larger, expansive fan base. Famous examples include *Abbott and Costello Meet Frankenstein, King Kong vs. Godzilla, Freddy vs. Jason*, and *The Avengers*.

Crossover, Audio, 2-Way Crossover. A group of digital filters used in the audio world to prevent signals from interfering with each other.

Crosstalk. In stereo, crosstalk is the irritating phenomenon in which an undesired signal in one audio channel will affect another channel.

Crowd Shot. A wide shot that covers a large group of people, like a rock concert or a massive rally. These shots are expensive, awesome, and time-consuming– that's showbiz!

Crushing the Blacks. This occurs when the shadows (or blacks) in an image become excessively dark, resulting in a loss of detail and definition. Ideally, this is done intentionally and not because your DP is overdue for an eye exam.

CT Filter. Dyed and heat resistant gel filters used to alter the color temperature of light. Typically attached to barn doors or gaff tape over LED lights. "CT" stands for Color Temperature.

CTB. Stands for "Color Temperature Blue."

CTO. Stands for "Color Temperature Orange."

CTS. Stands for "Color Temperature Straw."

CU, Close-up. A shot that's so up-close and personal, you feel like your face is right up against its subject. This is when the frame is filled with an object or person, giving us a detailed and intimate view of what's happening on screen. Just make sure your makeup team is watching the monitor.

Cue Cards. Actor's lines, written on oversized paper cards, or otherwise displayed, to assist in feeding lines to the performer. They're often used in fast paced late-night shows like SNL or *The Tonight Show*, or on any movie starring a particularly forgetful actor.

Cue Sheet. A list of copyrighted music used in a film. Cue sheets are a crucial part of the deliverables requested by the producer or distributor. It's important to get the music right, or your film might end up being the musical equivalent of a silent film.

Cue. The signal to do a specific action or say a certain line at a signaled time. An example would be, "throw the hot coffee in his face… on my cue."

Cult Film, Cult Classic. A film that has fans who are so dedicated, they have their own fan clubs. Famous examples include *A Clockwork Orange, Office Space, The Room,* and *Mean Girls.* There is typically some unique element to a cult film, whether that be a "so bad it's good" energy, or its incredible quotability, either way - you wanna watch it more than once!

Cup Blocks. Wooden blocks that hold the wheels of a lighting stand in place, keeping it from rolling away and knocking into something expensive (or alive). Also used to brace and support various other objects on a set.

Cut, Cutting. (1) Another word for an edit, or a version of a film. (2) The process of selecting and assembling the shots in a sequence. (3) That thing you're being forced to do because "your film is too damn long!".

Cut! A call made by a director at the end of each take to inform the end of a take. When the director calls "Cut!", it's time to take a break, check the gate and read more of this awesome dictionary glossary. It fits in your pocket!

Cutaway Shot. Cutting away from the main action of a scene to a single shot of something else, before cutting back to the original action. If you want to master the art of the cutaway shot, just watch an episode of *Arrested Development* and you'll learn everything you need to know.

Cutter, Fitter, Tailor. The person in charge of taking measurements and making alterations to garments for costuming. They make sure that the actors and actresses look their best, and their costumes are tailored to their bodies like they were made just for them (sometimes they are).

Cutter. A slang term for a film editor. They're the people who take all the footage and put it together to make the movie. Cutters are like the conductors of the movie orchestra, making sure every scene is in harmony and the movie hits all the right notes.

Cyc Lights. A special type of floodlight, used to illuminate and color the background evenly.

Cyclorama, Cyc Wall, Infinity Wall. A 360-degree panoramic platform that creates the appearance of a continuous background, typically found on big budget film sets. With advancements in technology, the Cyc walls have been replaced by Virtual Sets.

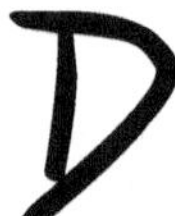

Dailies. Raw print or digital footage captured on the day, and ready for immediate view by the director. They're also known as Rushes, because you want to see them ASAP.

Dailies Colorist. Responsible for coloring and testing dailies.The Dailies Colorist works closely with dailies operators and producers to ensure timely delivery of deliverables.

Dailies Operator. Responsible for syncing, logging, rendering, and delivering the dailies.

Dance Choreographer, Choreographer. The creator and director of dance sequences, they design and direct the dance or stylized movement in musical productions.

Dark Current, Picture Noise. An ugly, pixelated image noise created by the absence of light, most commonly a result of incorrect ISO settings. It's reminiscent of those unrefined, flashless, intoxicated photos you took at that Limp Bizkit concert.

Dark Horse, Dark Horse Contender. A film that didn't receive much attention in the press or from audiences, and then received a nomination for a major award. Famous examples include *Rocky*, *Midnight Cowboy*, *The Exorcist* and that horror film you're working on. Yes, big things are coming your way!

DAT, Digital Audio Tape. The digital version of an audio cassette. It's a tape-based digital audio recording medium that's perfect for field recording. Not to be confused with the standard analog audio cassettes. How can a tape be digital you ask? Science! Is the answer.

Data Wrangler. The individual on set tasked with delivering the raw footage from the camera to the Editor, ensuring no damage or loss occurs. Given the critical nature of their job, it might be best to keep them away from that secret stash of booze we keep in the prop safe.

DaVinci Resolve. A color grading, color correction, VFX, and video editing application by Blackmagic Design. It truly is a one-stop-shop for all your post-production needs!

DAW, Digital Audio Workstation. A hardware/software system used for recording, editing and playing digital audio.

Day Out of Days, DOOD. A calendar-like chart used to calculate the number of paid days for each cast member prior to creating the film's budget. SAG is going to ask for it, so better have it ready.

Day Performer, SAG. A contractual SAG term that defines day rate compensation for an actor or performer. Day Performers receive payment per-day, as opposed to per-week.

Day Player. A crew member or cast member hired to work for just one day, or a few days (less than a standard work week). They're like the assassins of the film world. Come in, do their thing, and then disappear into the night.

Day-for-Night. Ah, the magic of filmmaking! This post-production process turns day into night, making your footage look like it was shot at night, even though it was shot in the middle of the day. What will they think of next?

Daylight Spool. An aluminum container used to protect film stock during a daylight camera load, keeping it from becoming exposed, like a 90s teenager's dad every time she's about to step out the door.

dB, Decibel. A unit of measurement for the intensity and loudness of a sound wave. Basically, sound is measured in decibels. A human whisper is around 30 dB, a car horn is 110 dB, a cat's meow is 45 dB, and an AD screaming at you to "Be quiet!" is off the damn charts at 130 bB.

DCP, Digital Cinema Package. A series of files required for digital cinema projection, mailed to a movie theater for quick ingestion. Just pop in the DCP and watch the cinema happen!

Dead Sync. When sound and picture are "perfectly synched." So, it's good.

Deal Memo. A short rundown of the agreed upon terms of a contract, typically including length of employment, salary, conditions, and other essentials for crew members and talent.

Decode. The digital process of reading and converting analog video signals to digital video.

Deconstruction. In film analysis, deconstruction is a literary or philosophical analysis of the relationship between text and meaning. It's a deep dive into the nitty-gritty details of what makes a movie more than just a series of scenes. It might sound pretentious as hell, but we just can't get enough of it!

Decoupage. In film editing, it's the process of laying out scenes in an order that illustrates the narrative progression of the film, but that does not necessarily follow the script. A method to convey, before a film is complete, the way it will look and feel.

Deep Focus. A cinematography technique of using a wide-angle lens with small apertures to produce a large depth of field and keep the entire image sharp, clear, and in focus. Director Orson Welles was a particular fan of this technique, and he popularized the deep focus technique in his 1941 classic *Citizen Kane*.

Deferee. A person to whom a deferment is payable. Just in case you needed to know that.

Deferment. Money payable at a later date. Deferment allows filmmakers to hold payment to cast and crew. This means the performers do not get paid until the terms of deferral are met. Scheduling payments this way makes it easier for filmmakers to fund their films and get into massive credit card debt.

Degausser. A device that eliminates recordings made on magnetic tapes. It's what your white collar criminal uncle Jeff used to permanently erase data from his hard drives.

Deleted scene. A scene that did not make the final cut of the film, often found in the DVD "bonus" section.

Deliverables. A collection of items required by a distributor or film festival to prepare a film for screening, release, marketing and distribution. You can't release a film without them!

Denouement. The final part of a narrative, usually following the climax, in which the story's conflicts are resolved and loose ends are tied up. It is often characterized by a sense of closure, as the various plot threads and character arcs come to a conclusion.

Density, Film Density. The amount of silver particles that are present in a photographic film emulsion, which determines the degree of opacity or transparency of the film. So, if you want a bold, contrasty and dramatic image, go for high density film. But if you're more of a low-contrast, subtle and nuanced person, low density film might be more your style. It's all about finding the right balance, baby!

Depth of Field, DOF. The area of an image that appears to be in focus. A shallow depth of field means that only a small portion of the image is in focus, while the rest appears blurred. This can be used to draw attention or to isolate a specific subject or object in the frame. A deep depth of field means that most or all of the image is in focus, from the foreground to the background. Depth of field is an important tool for filmmakers and photographers, as it can be used to create a sense of depth and dimensionality in an image, and to convey emotion or narrative information.

Designer. An artist responsible for designing materials such as posters, logos, wanted signs, and evil empire logos. Guess what? In your low-budget indie film, that person is most likely going to be you. So, it's high time to sign up for some Photoshop classes!

Developing. The process of converting unexposed film into a visible image. It's the "magic" part of the "magic of filmmaking."

Development Hell. It's when, despite every attempt to get a project off the ground, it ends up stuck in development for an especially long time, also known as Limbo. A few notable examples of movies that were in development hell for a few years are *Alita: Battle Angel, Deadpool, Avatar, Mad Max: Fury Road* , and that movie you've been trying to make since 2012.

Development, In Development. The pre-production phase where the director, along with several key team-members (typically ATL), works on the script, develops the characters, refines the overall look and feel of the film, as well as creates a budget and other necessities while waiting for a greenlight. It's the second step in the production process, right after disappointing a writer with a draconian contract.

DGA, Director's Guild of America. A labor union which represents directors, assistant directors, production managers, and various video personnel.

DI Finishing Artist, Finishing Artist. A skilled professional responsible for color correction, image enhancement, and finalizing the look of a film or TV show. They meticulously sculpt the final visual aesthetic of a shot. Not to be confused with Colorist.

Dialect Coach. Dialect coaches are the ones who teach actors how to speak and sound like their characters, making sure that their accents fit the world of the film. We've all seen a movie where the accents are ridiculous, distracting and laughable; dialect coaches help avoid that.

Dialogue Editor. A sound editor whose focus is purely on dialogue. Tasks include the assembly, synchronization, and editing of all the dialogue in a production, making it as clear as possible for the sound editor. It's painstaking work but someone has to do it!

Dialogue Track. A separate audio track consisting exclusively of the film's dialogue.

Diegetic Sound. Sound effects that appear to come from on-screen action, created by something within the film, like a character's voice or the sound a car makes when the key is turned in the ignition. This is opposed to, for instance, the score or any ambient effects…or the sound of the filmmaker crying in the back of the screening room because his/her film sounds like poop.

Difference Key, Difference Matte Key, Key. A method of separating a subject from its background by extracting matte information in post-production. A key concept in blue screen and green screen VFX. ^{See, Matte.}

Diffusion, Diff. The process of using a diffuser or translucent sheet to soften harsh light.

Digital Asset Management, DAM. The process of organizing, storing, retrieving, and distributing digital assets in a way that maximizes their value and efficiency. DAM systems are designed to centralize all digital assets in a single location, making it easier to find and access them for editing.

Digital Compositor. A visual effects person responsible for compositing, duh!

Digital Imaging Technician, DIT. A person responsible for image quality control, on-set color correction, and managing a production's workflow.

Digital Intermediate, DI. The process of digitizing a film, color correcting it, "finishing it", and re-outputting it to film before it is ready for distribution.

Digital Negative, DNG. An open, raw image format created by Adobe.

Digital Production. A movie-shoot using digital cameras instead of film. They still call it filmmaking, even though there's no "film" involved. "I'm making a film" has a better ring to it than, "I'm making a digital movie."

Digital Sculptors. A VFX artist whose job is to create high-quality, digital 3D surface models for use by the film's VFX department. Typically by use of Z-Brush or other super complicated sculpting software.

Digital Theatre Systems, DTS, Digital Theater Systems. A company that specializes in creating digital surround sound formats for use in film and home theater systems. Not to be confused with Dolby, which uses a compression method to encode multiple audio channels into a single bitstream. DTS uses a higher bit rate and less compression to achieve its surround sound format, which is often regarded as having higher sound quality than Dolby Digital.

Digital Zoom. An in-camera and/or post-production process of automatically cropping a portion of a digital image to produce a zoom effect.

Digitize. The process of preparing analog video for a digital edit by converting it to a digital format– just in case you wondered how your parent's SD wedding video made its way onto your mom's Facebook page.

Dim it Down. A request to lower a light's intensity, either because it's too bright or because we're still hungover from last night's wrap.

Dimmer. A device for modulating the intensity of a light.

Diopter. A lens attachment that serves as a magnifying glass, allowing a non-macro lens to capture macro shots. Also, can refer to the adjustable portion of a view-finding system.

Direct Sound. The method of using one piece of equipment (such as a camera) to record both the audio and visual simultaneously, as opposed to using multiple devices. Just make sure you don't accidentally plug your shotgun mic into the headphones jack. It'll be hilarious, but also very sad.

Directing the eye. (1) The process of using camera, light and framing to draw the audience's eye where you want it to go; to compel viewers to pay attention to something significant on-screen. (2) The process of directing the actor's eye movement for the purpose of matching eyelines or achieving a certain dramatic effect.

Directional Characteristics. The variation of sound based on the microphone's position and angle.

Director of Photography, DP, DOP. Another term for Cinematographer.

Director. The creative force behind the making of a movie. They are responsible for bringing the script to life and realizing the vision of the film. They oversee all aspects of the filmmaking process, from pre-production to post-production.

Director's Cut. A contractual clause giving a director final say on how the film will ultimately be edited. While it may sound hard to get, we have faith in you. Go get it!

Dirt. Slang for sandbag, a bag filled with sand used on a film set to stabilize equipment, such as light stands and tripod legs, and to prevent them from tipping over.

Discovery Shot. Term to describe when the camera moves to reveal a person or object in the scene that was not previously disclosed to the viewer. This shot is used often on *It's Always Sunny in Philadelphia*.

Dissolve. An editing transition in which one shot seems to fade into the next.

Distortion. An intentional or unintentional modification made to the original video or audio signal.

Distribution Agreement. An agreement granting a distributor the rights to sell the film. It's what every filmmaker wants at the end of the day – for the film to find a good home with a semi-reputable distributor who won't rip them off as much. #LifeGoals #DreamBig

Distributor. The company responsible for organizing and coordinating the marketing, exhibition, and distribution of a finished film to its intended audience. Your movie will die in obscurity without them.

Ditty Bag. A grab-and-go tool bag used to store camera and lens essentials.

DME Mix, Music and Effects Mix. The film's final audio mix which includes all sound channels (effects, foley, music, etc.) with the exception of the dialogue track. Used when dubbing a film in a foreign language.

DMP, Digital Matte Painter. The Digital Matte Painter (DMP) creates photorealistic digital matte painting environments for feature films; often for fantasies, sci-fi films and big epics. See, Matte Paintings.

Documentary. A non-fiction film that reports on a real subject, often a true story, though it may sometimes be biased. Typically involves a sweaty filmmaker screaming at unsuspecting politicians on the steps of the White House, something I'll always pay good money to see.

Dogme 95. A 1995 filmmaking manifesto by Danish directors Lars von Trier and Thomas Vinterberg, in which they urged their fellow filmmakers to resist pressure from studios to make films based on special effects. They hoped to encourage a return to filmmaking that emphasized art, individual expression, and storytelling focused on human struggles and humanist values. Thank God that took off!

Dolby 5.1. A six channel digital surround sound system by Dolby encompassing five speakers and one subwoofer for bass.

Dolby Stereo. A digital audio encoding system created by Dolby in 1976

Dolly Grip. A grip crewmember responsible for operating dollies and cranes. If you think *you're* hot, try pushing a dolly carrying two grownups and a 60 pound camera on a track.

Dolly Tracks. A set of tracks upon which a camera dolly is mounted, typically removed from the box truck then immediately put back after the director changes his mind.

Dolly Zoom, Zolly, The Vertigo Shot. An optical effect created by dollying the camera towards or away from the subject while turning a zoom lens in the opposite direction to achieve a perspective distortion where the background appears to shrink or expand relative to the subject. It's a shot made famous by *Vertigo*, *Jaws*, and *Goodfellas*.

Dolly, Dolly Shot. A smooth motion or tracking shot in which the camera is mounted on a dolly.

Domestic Rights. The rights to distribute a film in North America, or wherever your film/production company is based.

Domestic, Gross Domestic. Referring to domestic box office ticket sales.

DOOD Report. Another term for Day Out of Days. A hart used to calculate the number of paid days for each cast member prior to creating the film's budget. SAG is going to ask for it, so better have it ready.

Doorway Dolly. A dolly that is sufficiently narrow so as to fit through a doorway.

Dope Sheet. (1) A detailed list of every scene and shot created in an animated or CG film. (2) A very comfortable sheet. #ThreadCountsCount

Dots. Small flags used to manipulate light.

Double Bill, Double Feature. Two movies shown sequentially, at a discounted admission price. The first film being the major attraction (the A Movie), and the second film being typically less of a pull (the B Movie). This practice became popular during the Great Depression in the early 1930s, and lasted through WWII, only to make a resurgence in 2023 during Barbenheimer.

Double Exposure. The process of exposing a single frame twice to produce an awesome ghostly effect, popular in '80s music videos and low budget horror films.

Double-System Sound. The method of recording sound and picture on separate devices and synchronizing them later in post-production. The opposite of Direct Sound. It's how most movies are made!

Double, Stunt-Double. A highly-skilled person trained to perform difficult and dangerous choreography/stunts; hired to substitute actors in physically demanding scenes that are considered unsafe. It helps a lot if you look like The Rock.

Down-conversion. The process of converting HD (High Def) to SD (Low Def).

DPX, Digital Picture Exchange. A high-end file sequence format for use in digital intermediate and VFX. So, please, don't send your VFX artist an AVI file.

Draftsman. A trained drawing artist who interprets and sketches set construction plans. If you've ever stepped foot inside an Imperial landing craft and wondered, "who's the architect?" - it's that person!

Dresser. An on-set wardrobe assistant who helps actors make costume changes and helps in the upkeep and organization of the garments.

Drive-in. A drive-in is an outdoor movie theater where viewers pay to park their cars in a large parking lot to watch films projected onto an enormous screen. (This also provides an opportunity to make out with their crush in the privacy of a dimly lit parking lot.) Drive-ins gained popularity in the '60s, when a growing number of Americans were becoming car owners, moving to the suburbs, and land was inexpensive.

Driver. A crew member (often Teamster) responsible for transporting people and equipment between sets and locations as needed. They're also known for imposing their playlist on captive audiences for hours on end.

Drone Photographer, Drone Op, Drone Operator. Responsible for operating drones in order to capture cinematic aerial shots without the need for a helicopter. Because... technology!

Drop Frame. A form of timecode in which two frames are dropped every minute. A frame drop is when a video or film skips one or more frames, resulting in a momentary interruption in the playback either because of a bad connection or crummy wi-fi.

Dropout. (1) A sudden drop in signal resulting in the loss of data or excess noise. (2) A person who never finished film school.

DSLR, Digital Single Lens Reflex. A single lens reflex digital camera that captures high res images and video.

Dub Stage, Mix Stage, The Dub. A theater-like environment designed for creating the film's final sound-mix.

Dub. To add a new, dubbed dialogue track on top of the film's M&E track. Used when selling the film to territories that speak a different language than the original film and where the preference is for audio over subtitles. Just in case you wanted to know what your actors sounded like in Japanese!

Dubber. A magnetic playback unit with exceptional sound reproduction quality. Often used in IMAX Sound Systems.

Dubbing. The process of synching an actor's voice with the lip movements of the actor who is seen speaking on screen during ADR.

Dumb Side. Looking in the direction of the camera/lens, instead of right at it.

Dunning. The method of combining and matching studio shots with footage shot on location. It's an invaluable part of movie magic.

Dupe. A copy of a negative. Short for Duplicate.

Dutch Tilt, Dutch Angle, Canting. A shot in which the camera is tilted diagonally at a canted angle, it's tilted to one side, resulting in a diagonal composition of the frame.

Duvetyne. A heavy black cloth used for blocking light, blacking out windows, hiding cables, etc. You can never have enough of this stuff on set, so… invest wisely.

DV. A Standard Definition (SD) data format with a resolution of 640x480 / 720x480.

DVD. A Digital Versatile Disc. An optical disc format for recording and replaying a movie. Something millennials know well but anyone born after the year 2010 will have a hard time understanding. Hey! At least it's not a Laserdisc!

Dynamic Frame. The post production process of fitting a frame into the appropriate ratio. You could call it that, or just tell the editor to "resize it please."

Dynamic Range, Image. The difference between the brightest and darkest parts of an image. Measured in "stops," each stop indicates a doubling of the level of brightness captured. The human eye can see up to 20 stops of dynamic range, RED Gemini around 16, and film somewhere between 12 and 15 stops.

Dynamic Range, Sound. The decibel difference between the loudest and quietest portions of a recorded sound.

Dystopia. A fictional world or society that is characterized by extreme suffering, oppression, and often a total lack of freedom or individuality (in other words, North Korea!). It is a genre of science fiction that portrays a bleak future, usually caused by some kind of catastrophic event, societal collapse, or authoritarian regime. Dystopian films include *Mad Max*, *Children of Men*, *Equilibrium*, and *Minority Report*.

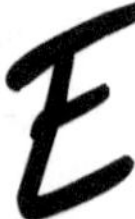

Earn Out. Ah, the illustrious "Earn Out" - that magical moment in the film industry when a project finally recoups its costs and starts making a profit.

Easter Egg. A delightful event, object or character in a film that might be too subtle to be noticed on the first watch. It's a little extra something that makes the whole movie watching experience a little more enjoyable, and it's what comic book movies do best!

Echo. An effect produced by the reflection of sound waves from a surface. It's what you get when you yell profanities into a cave.

ECU. An abbreviation for Extreme Closeup.

Edge Numbers. Numbers printed along the edges of a strip of film which allow the negative cutter to keep track of and identify frames.

Edge Track. The standard position for audio placement on magnetic film.

Edit Decision List, EDL. A digital list created by an offline editing system like Premiere or Resolve used during post-production. The list contains the order of the cut sequence stipulated by the editor.

Edit Master. The precious tape containing the film's final cut. Keep it safe, in a safe.

Edit Points. The beginning and end points of an edit.

Editing bench. Another term for Editing Room, whether that be in a professional post production studio or in your grandmother's basement.

Editing. The art, technique, and practice of selecting and assembling raw footage to make a coherent and compelling sequence. The editing process is the final stage in which the film is constructed.

Editor. Technical artists responsible for selecting the perfect takes and piecing them together to create a masterpiece. Working closely with the director, the editor helps bring their vision to life by weaving together a cohesive story that grips the audience from start to finish.

Effective Output Level. The strength or power of an audio signal after it has been processed by a piece of audio equipment, such as a mixer or amplifier.

Effects Animation. The control over on-screen particle VFX elements such as explosions, smoke, fire and rain. It's what the X-Men and the Transformers do best!

Effects Stock. High-quality 35mm film stock optimized for shooting visual effects. Because we all love the word "high quality."

Electrical Department. The department responsible for light and electrical wiring on set. They truly put the E in G&E, or the "spark" in circuit testers, voltage detectors, and clamp meters.

Electrician. A grip responsible for handling the distribution of electricity on-set, from cameras and monitors, to lights, computers, faulty walkies, and coffee makers.

Electronic Viewfinder, EVF. A digital viewfinder. A small window on the camera body that allows the photographer to see through the lens and frame the shot they want to capture. as opposed to looking at a smudgy, fingerprint heavy monitor.

Ellipsis. (1) A plot device used to keep important sections of the narrative hidden from the audience. (2) That thing your screenwriter friend uses way too much of… #ScreenwritingTropes

ELS. Another term for Extreme Long Shot; a type of camera shot that shows a wide view of a large area, such as a landscape or cityscape, with the subject appearing small and distant, like your love life.

Emulsion. A light-sensitive coating on film which, when exposed to light, undergoes a chemical change that allows images to appear. It's the "magic" element in the "magic of filmmaking."

Encode. The process of writing video information onto a new file, generally for compression or to meet deliverable requirements by a distributor, an exhibitor, or… you know, YouTube. #No-Judgement

End Crawl. Final credit sequence, also known as End Credits, The Crawl, Closing Credits, Rear-Title Crawl, Scrolling End Credits, and That Thing They Misspelled Your Name In.

Ensemble, Ensemble Cast, Ensemble Work. A group of actors at the center of a film who, together, are the collective "star" of the film. So… they all deserve a trailer, add it to the budget. Examples include *Nashville*, *Boogie Nights*, and *Pulp Fiction*.

Entertainment Lawyer. Lawyers who specialize in the entertainment industry. They are the glue that keeps the film industry from collapsing into a legal nightmare where everyone is suing each other all the time, and they do it by use of costly contracts, expensive phone calls, and script notes that no one asked for.

Entertainment Value. A film's capacity to entertain. High entertainment value is not that hard to conjure, all you need is an amazing script, an entertaining cast of marvelous actors, a great director, an even better editor. See? easy.

Envelope. (1) In sound design, it's the amplitude of a sound wave over time. (2) That thing you get in the mail and then immediately throw in the trash.

Environmental Sound. The background sounds and noises that exist within a scene or location, such as traffic, birds chirping, or people talking in the distance.

Environmental Steward. Responsible for reducing the amount of waste produced on set.

Epic. A big budget film, often produced on a massive scale with heavy VFX, stunts, an A-list cast, and enough crafty to feed a hungry nation for a month.

Epilogue. A concluding scene or sequence in a film reflecting upon the conclusion of the story. It gives viewers who liked the film a sense of closure, and those who hated it a chance to go to the bathroom before the crowds come spilling out of the theater.

Epiphany. When a character suddenly realizes something important, like when your mom finally realizes the name of that actor she likes– Channing Tatum, mom, it's Channing Tatum.

Episode. An hour or half-hour long segment in a television series.

Episodic. A TV series or Limited Series that takes place over time and/or episodes.

EPK, Electronic Press Kit. The film industry's version of a "show and tell." It's a file (digital or printed) containing a treasure trove of goodies designed to entice members of the media to cover your film. An EPK will typically feature stuff like production notes, bios, still images, posters, trailer links, and all sorts of juicy details about the film. It's the ultimate cheat sheet for journalists and critics who want to know everything there is to know about the movie before praising (or destroying) it in the media. Aren't you happy you sent it?

Equalization, EQ. It's the post-production process of balancing out all the sound frequencies so you can hear the dialogue over the sweet sounds of a heavy-breathing boom operator.

Equipment Coordinator. Works with the Line Producer and field crews to prepare, pack, ship, test and maintain equipment on set. It's the person who makes sure the camera is there. Kinda hard to shoot the film without it.

Errors & Omissions Insurance, E&O. A type of insurance policy that protects the producers and distributors from liability suits, like that time you accidentally forgot to clear the rights to that Elvis Presley song. Oops.

Establishing Shot. A shot intended to establish a location and the time of day, for example: Wide Shot, Above Ground Sex Dungeon - Day. You're welcome.

EVF. Abbreviation for an Electronic Viewfinder. It lets you see what you're filming without having to stare at the monitor.

Exchangeable Image File, EXIF. A file format used for storing metadata.

Exciter Lamp. A specialized projector bulb that emits light through a film's soundtrack, which then triggers a photoelectric cell to create current fluctuations that ultimately produce sound through a loudspeaker.

Executive Producer, EP. A producer who represents the film production company or an investor responsible for financing the movie. They typically handle the business and legal aspects of the production. Executive Producers can often be film investors, loan brokers, financiers, or your parents - after you've begged them for $500 to realize your short film dream.

Executive Summary. A document created by the production to illustrate the business end of the film. Often used during fundraising and pitching. Because even a ridiculous movie about a murderous potato coming to life needs a business plan.

Exhibitor. A fancy word for a movie theater or drive-in; the place where dreams are made, over-priced popcorn is sold, and car batteries come to die.

Expendables. Secondary or support gear. You think you don't need it, but they'll still make you pay for it.

Experimental Film. An artistic film genre representing the director's pure artistic vision without consideration for marketability or audience.

Exploitation Film. A subgenre of B movies that seeks to exploit taboo (most often racial, sexual, violent, or vulgar) themes. They can be fun to watch, with the right audience.

Export. When you finally hit that "Render" button and let your precious video out of the editing software nest and into the big, wide world for people to judge. A process fraught with log waiting times, too much coffee, and computers heating up and crashing at 99.76%.

Exposition. Background information that might or might not be necessary to the advancement or understanding of a storyline. It can be used wisely (*The Social Network's* "It's raining."), or abused terribly ("Oh my God, look over there!! It's him!! My cousin that went to jail three years ago for murder! He's got a knife! No!!!!!"). Sometimes less is more.

Exposure Compensation. The technique of adding to or subtracting exposure levels to produce an either darker or brighter image, because lights are expensive, y'all.

Exposure Index. A way of measuring how light-sensitive a particular type of film or sensor is. Like a vampire in the sun, some film stocks just can't take the heat.

Exposure. The amount of light passing through the lens aperture and striking the surface of film or the digital imaging sensor. Exposure levels dictate how bright or dark your shot will be. Expose too much, and your picture will be burnt toast. Too little, and you'll be left with the *Game of Thrones* finale.

Expressionism. A film style that uses distortion or exaggeration of visual elements to reflect inner feelings and emotions of a character or filmmaker. Might also refer to German Expressionism. Examples include *Destiny*, *Nosferatu*, and *The Cabinet of Dr. Caligari*.

EXT, Exterior. In screenplays, EXT is used to indicate a scene taking place outdoors. So pack your picnic basket Sally, we're going to shoot in the park tomorrow!

Extension Tubes. A hollow metal lens-mount tube used to turn a regular long lens into a macro lens for ultra-close shooting. It's technology, it's science, and it's a thing you buy at B&H for $79.99.

Extra. An actor or performer appearing on-screen who is not a member of the cast and does not have any lines. Can be a Background Extra (used in the background) or a Featured Extra (used in a tight shot, visible on-screen). They're the ones who wait in makeshift tents while the stars hide in their trailers.

Extreme Close-up, ECU. A very tight, detailed shot in which the subject is much larger than the frame. Best used when you want to see every wrinkle, pore, and nose hair in stunning detail.

Eye Light, Catchlight. A light that creates a small sparkle reflected in a person's eyes to make them look extra alive. It's an artform unto itself.

Eyeline Match. A film editing technique that establishes or reveals the subject at which the character is shown to be looking.

Eyeline, "What's My Eyeline?". A question you often get as a film director; it's when the actor needs to know where to look, either in-frame or off-frame. Eyeline needs to make sense, so it's important to get it right. Yet another reason for why you shouldn't do drugs before showing up to work!

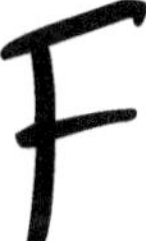

F-Stop. A term used to describe the lens aperture and measure how much light passes through it and onto the sensor. The lower the stop, the brighter the image and shallower the depth of field (more stuff out of focus), the higher the stop, the darker the image and crispier the image (everything's in focus!). I think we got it.

FAST (Focus, Aperture, Shutter, Tachometer). The 1st AC's four critical responsibilities. <u>Focus</u> refers to the precise sharpness and clarity of the image, while <u>Aperture</u> relates to the size of the opening in the lens. <u>Shutter</u> speed determines the length of time the camera's sensor is exposed to light, and <u>Tachometer</u> refers to the measurement of the camera's motor speed.

Fade. A measured, gradual transition from one shot to another, or in the case of "Fade to Black," to black.

Fake Shemp. Colloquial term for a stand-in. When the star is too busy sipping lattes, it's time to call in the stand-in.

False Color. A monitor feature that reads exposure levels in a shot. The levels are presented in different colors to help the cinematographer adjust light, exposure, brightness, and color. False Color is the monitor's way of admitting that it's lying to you.

Fay, Molefay. A form of light used to replicate sunlight. For those days when the sun opts to hide behind a cloud, Fay got you covered.

Feather Light, Light Feathering. The technique of manipulating a soft-box light so that only a desired area of the shot is illuminated.

Feather. A post-production technique used for blurring and softening the edges of a frame, light source, or digital mask. It's the editor's way of softening their "fix it in post" effect so that you can't tell that they fixed it in post.

Feature Film. The OG of movies - any narrative film offering 40 minutes or longer of cinematic gold. Fun fact - the first feature film ever made was the 1906 Australian Western, *The Story of the Kelly Gang*.

Feature Presentation, Main Attraction. The main or advertised film being exhibited in a double feature, also called the Á movie. It's the moment you've been waiting for, also the moment you finally realize what the B in B movie stood for. Who would have guessed?

Featured Background. Featured extras placed strategically in a scene.

Featurette. A short film that's not as long as a feature, but not as short as a short. Anything over 25 minutes, really. Maybe it's time to consider cutting it down a bit.

Feed Lines. Lines of dialogue read to an actor off-screen, often when they can't bother with their memorizing lines. So, we "feed" the actors their lines, ugh.

Feel-Good Film. A light-hearted film in which the purpose is to put a smile on your face and make you feel all cozy inside. Examples include *Legally Blonde*, *Paddington*, *Zoolander*, and *Clueless*.

Femme Fatale. A seductive and dangerous female character; the ultimate man-eater. Famous examples include Kathryn Merteuil in *Cruel In-*

tentions, Phyllis Dietrichson in *Double Indemnity*, and Jennifer Check in *Jennifer's Body*.

Festival, Film Festival. An event organized to promote, introduce and celebrate motion pictures. Festivals give platforms to both professional and amateur filmmakers alike. It's a place where you can discover new films and make new friends, and brag to your family members about that time you almost ran into Andy Dick at the Fort Wayne Film Festival.

FICA. The U.S. federal payroll tax, deducted from paychecks across all industries. It's the government's way of saying, "Hey, congrats on getting paid! Gimme it!" In film accounting, it is typically accounted for under the "Fringes" category, and no - it's not the fringe you're living in.

Field Monitor. A large-screen alternative to the tiny on-camera LCD screen. Field monitors allow sweaty crew-members to huddle together on top of each other to see whatever the camera is capturing. It's like having your own personal movie theater on set, where you and your crew can watch your masterpiece unfold in real time.

Fifteen Minutes. A short-lived celebrity, typically hated and belittled by those who never had *any* minutes of fame.

Fight Choreographer. The person responsible for designing the action sequence of a fight scene so that it appears to be real, but is also well-rehearsed and safe. Keeping the actors and stunt performers safe from getting punched in the face is an important job, someone's gotta do it!

File Format. The way in which files (audio, VFX, image, video, etc) are saved and stored.

Fill Light, Fill. A supplementary tool used to lighten and soften shadows, often a light, reflector, or bounce. A type of lighting (or a lighting tool) used to control the contrast in an image by filling in shadows and reducing the harshness created by the key light.

Film Aesthetics. The study of film as a visual art form. The theoretical debate and judgment about what film as an art form can achieve as well as the criteria it must meet to be judged as "successful" in this philosophical context.

Film Artifact. The damage or defect found on a piece of film, caused by some external, unplanned factor.

Film Base. A transparent material which acts as support for a film's photographic emulsions.

Film Buyer, Acquisition Executive. (1) A movie studio representative responsible for acquiring the rights to independently-produced films. They're the people you want to have in your contact list!! (2) A movie studio employee responsible for buying, stocking and reselling film stock.

Film Cement. A common term for the welding solvent used to melt and fuse two pieces of film together.

Film Clip. A visual snippet, often used to promote the film during its release.

Film Developing. The process of developing film stock and transferring the footage to a negative print.

Film Editor. The person responsible for putting the film together in post-production.

Film Form. A critical term referencing the sum of all the moving elements and literary devices which make up a completed scene or a finished film, and the perceivable relationship between them.

Film Gauge. The width measurement of the film strip, e.g., 8mm, 35mm, 16mm, etc.

Film Grain. The random texture of processed film caused by the presence of small particles on the film strip. Film grain is often added to digital movies in post-production in order to give them a "film-like" aesthetic. Because we all want to keep "film" alive, right?

Film Loader, Clapper-Loader. A crew-member responsible for loading film magazines and managing film inventory. They also typically operate the clapper-board, it's all in the name.

Film Magazine. A reel of fresh film stock ready for use in a camera.

Film Noir, Noir. A genre of black and white, high-contrast film prevalent mostly in American crime dramas of the post World War II era. Noir's most recognizable features include cynical heroes, sharp dialogue, long-winded flashbacks, and sexy femme fatales smoking cigarettes and single-tear crying in private detective offices. It's awesome! Examples include *Double Indemnity*, *Out of the Past*, *The Third Man*, and *The Big Sleep*.

Film Plane, Sensor Plane. The flat surface of the sensor (or film) where the lens creates the focused image. The Plane Indicator is a visual reference designed to inform focus pullers where the plane in the camera is located.

Film Printing. The process of transferring film from a negative print to a Release Print; it's when a film is ready for print!

Film Review. A published evaluation of a film's appeal and quality by a credentialed (or non-credentialed) professional; usually a newspaper writer, film critic, or your drunk uncle talking about how much he hated *Avatar*.

Film Riot. A popular, DIY filmmaking web series hosted by the incomparable Ryan Connolly and his gang of awesome family members.

Film Speed. The light-sensitivity index of motion picture film or digital camera sensors. Film speed refers to the measure of a film's sensitivity to light. The lower the speed of the film, the more light is needed to create the desired image.

Film Stock. Ready-to-shoot film.

Film within a Film. A storytelling device where a fictional movie is created within the context of the main movie's plot. It's often full of awesome easter eggs for filmmakers and fans of the craft. But it's also a way for filmmakers to provide commentary on the film industry itself. Examples include *Tropic Thunder, Zack and Miri Make a Porno, Once Upon a Time in Hollywood.*

Film. (1) A series of moving images captured on film stock and played back at 24FPS. (2) A thin strip or transparent sheet over the film negative that makes images visible when exposed to light. (3) A term referring to a movie or motion picture.

Filmmaker. A brave soul who takes on the Herculean task of bringing a story to life on film. The term can apply to anyone gutsy enough to put a film together. It's a job that requires a unique combination of skills and traits: creativity, vision, patience, leadership, and perhaps most importantly, a healthy dose of "balls to the wall crazy". But despite the many trials and tribulations of filmmaking, the end result is often more than worth the trip.

Filmography. A list of films created by a single person (actor, director, producer) or company, or a list of unrelated films that all address the same topic.

Filter. (1) Any glass or plastic sheet that can be inserted in the optical path to alter or affect an image in some way. (2) A software add-on used to reproduce a desired effect digitally. (3) Any material used to absorb light, color or sound. (4) That thing you add on your Instagram photos to make it look like you're having fun at the gym.

Final Cut. The "final" edited and polished version of a film that will be released for viewing.

Final Cut Pro. An editing software by Apple that used to be awesome.

Fingers. Small flags used to manipulate light.

Firewire. A high-speed data transfer standard.

Firmware. In-device software containing various features and options. Helps keep your camera and bluetooth devices up to date.

First Assistant Camera, 1st AC. The trusty sidekick to the Camera Operator, helping them keep shots in focus and avoid blurry nightmares; they also set up and maintain camera equipment, stabilize gimbals, and load/unload film (or memory cards).

First Assistant Director, First AD. A key member of the filmmaking team responsible for ensuring the efficient and smooth running of the production. Their primary responsibilities include creating the shooting schedule, overseeing the day-to-day operations on set, coordinating the cast and crew, ensuring that the director's vision is realized on-screen, and making sure the actors don't freak out because of a late lunch hour. The 1st AD is often considered the "right hand" of the director, and their ability to keep the production running on time and within budget is critical to the success of the film. Sounds like an important hire, doesn't it?

First Trial Print. A synonym for the Answer Print. The first lab-produced copy made from the negative.

Fish Out of Water. A premise for a story in which the main character is placed in a completely unfamiliar, even strange and unfriendly, environment with the intention of creating conflict and often, humor. Prime examples include *Beverly Hills Cop*, *My Cousin Vinny*, *Coneheads*, and *Legally Blonde*.

Fish-Eye. A distorted ultra wide-angle lens used to produce wide, panoramic or hemispherical shots. Its unique shape produces a distinctive distortion effect, making everything look like it's been stretched and warped in all sorts of wacky ways.

Fitting. A costume fitting/wardrobe test. Often conducted with the actors in advance of the film's first day of shooting, because when the clothes don't fit, bad (and hilarious) things happen.

Fix it in Post. (1) A phrase for when a shot has a manageable mess-up that could be concealed or fixed during the post-production process. (2) A sarcastic comment about the current state of an amateur shoot, often punctuated with a massive eye-roll and a depressed director sulking in the corner.

Fixed Focal Length Lens. Another term for a Prime Lens. A type of camera lens that has a fixed focal length, meaning it cannot zoom in or out. These lenses typically have a wider maximum aperture than zoom lenses, allowing for more light to enter the camera and resulting in sharper and more detailed images.

Fixing. The removal of unexposed silver halides (light-sensitive compounds that react with light to form images) from a film during processing.

Flag on the Play. After concluding a take, someone realizes there was a problem with the shot and it needs to be redone. Because that's always fun!

Flag. (1) A type of black cloth used to manipulate light and shadow. (2) A small rectangular or square-shaped accessory that attaches to the front of a matte box on a camera lens, designed to block out unwanted light from entering the camera lens.

Flare, Lens Flare. A lens artifact caused by light, or in post in a J.J. Abrams film.

Flash frame. The method of inserting a single frame into a sequence with the intent of producing a sudden dramatic effect, popularized by *Fight Club* and copied by hungry artists worldwide.

Flash-Forward. The narrative device in which a future event is shown to shed light on what is happening on the screen in the present. So... the opposite of a flashback.

Flash-in-the-Pan. Overnight success or sudden and perhaps, fleeting recognition. It's what the Hollywood dream is all about!... Ain't it?

Flashback. A jump back to an earlier time – either within the narrative timeframe or further back in the characters' past – to illuminate some event that has an effect on the story at present.

Flat Profile. A low contrast, low sharpness picture profile meant to replicate a cinema camera color space; for those times when you cannot afford a cinema camera, but want to pretend that you have one nonetheless.

Flex-Fill. A round cloth collapsible reflector. It's like having a portable light reflector in your pocket. Good luck de-collapsing it back into shape, it's comedy.

Flick. A colloquial term for a movie uttered by old people, thought to be derived from the early 20th century, when films "flickered" as they were projected in a dark theater.

Flicker. A strobing effect produced by fluorescent lighting and visible in slow motion film. Fluorescent bulbs use high voltage pulses to create luminescence. These pulses happen so quickly that our eyes don't notice them, but cameras do. To avoid this, use an incandescent bulb or shoot in natural sunlight. Or, you know, just embrace the funky disco vibes!

Float. Undesired image movements caused by a faulty camera or projector.

Flood. A powerful light used to illuminate a large section of the set or a street. They're expensive, big, and awesome.

Flop, Bomb, Box-Office Bomb. An expensive movie that fails to recoup its production costs and often trigger a financial disaster for the studio dumb enough to back it. While there are many reasons a movie can bomb—be it marketing, casting, or release timing—sometimes, it's just because the movie is just plain terrible, and nobody wants to subject themselves to such cinematic torture. We're looking at you, *Mars Needs Moms*.

Flop, Flips. The effect of reversing an image horizontally. Why? Just... because.

Floppy. (1) A large flag with an extra flap that is held in place with hook-and-loop fabric. (2) An old computer disk meant to store files, a popular trope in '90s films.

Flux. The measurement of the perceived power of a particular light source.

Flying In, Fly In. A person or object brought physically into the set. ("Flying her in, now!")

Flyover, Flyover Audience. (1) A literal, though pejorative description of the millions of people who live between New York and California, as seen looking downward from a coast-to-coast flight, by producers and executives who need the flyover audience to make their film successful. (2) The taste of viewers who are considered unsophisticated by NY and LA standards. Because that's not pretentious at all.

Foamcore. Lightweight material used to create reflectors, soft boxes, and other items.

Focal Length Magnifier, Crop Factor. The ratio of a digital camera's focal length dimensions (the distance between the lens and the image sensor where light is focused to form a sharp image) compared to a 35mm format.

Focus Group, Test Screening. A sneak-preview screening of a film to a targeted audience who are selected because they have no stake in the movie. In some cases, changes are made to the film in response to a strong reaction from a film's test screening. In other cases, film directors insist that the movie is FINE! While test scores reflect the sad realities which they refuse to acknowledge. This is a fun industry full of awesome personalities.

Focus Pull, Focus Puller. The process of refocusing the lens during a shot to keep an object or subject in focus, or to manually change the camera's point of focus. This should be done by the Focus Puller, who presumably knows what he/she is doing, otherwise you risk lamenting a shot you can't use because it's out of focus.

Focus Ring. (1) A ring on a lens which is manually or automatically rotated to achieve the exact degree of focus needed. (2) An add-on ring, fitted on top of a standard photography lens to make it function like a cinema lens, giving the focus puller the same degree of control over the focus.

Focus. (1) The degree of visible sharpness or clarity of an object, subject or background in an image. (2) That thing you say to yourself in the mirror before going back to set after everyone saw you cry in the corner.

Fog Level. The minimum density of the unexposed area of processed film.

Fog Machine, Smoke Machine, Haze Machine. Devices used to emit a misty or foggy atmosphere, enhancing the mood and ambience of a scene. The machine heats up a special fluid, which is then expelled into the air as a fine mist. This creates a hazy effect that can be illuminated by lights on set. If you ever have a character walking with a flashlight in a dark room, you'll be thankful you have that hazer running!

Foley Artist. An artist responsible for producing and recording sound effects for a film. They use various objects and surfaces to mimic the sounds of footsteps, doors opening and closing, clothing rustling, and any other sound that could enhance the feel of a scene.

Foley Editor, Foley Mixer. A sound editor in-charge of editing the sound effects produced by a Foley Artist.

Foley. A sound design process of fabricating, reproducing, recording, and synching character-related sound effects such as footsteps, cloth-noise, breathing, fighting, crying, dying, and exploding.

Follow Focus. A focus control mechanism, commonly a part of a rig, attached to the lens's focus ring that allows the focus puller to, you know… pull focus.

Follow Shot, Tracking Shot. A smooth and steady shot that follows or tracks a moving subject or object; it's why you spent that $700 on that Ronin you hate.

Foot Candle. A way of measuring light. One foot candle equals the volume of light produced by a single candle, as seen from one foot away.

Footage. Any visual portion of a film or digital sequence, i.e., a video or film clip. You can't make a movie without it!

Forced Perspective. The optical illusion that makes an object appear bigger or smaller than it actually is. It's the reason why your aunt can appear to be holding up the Leaning Tower of Pisa, or why Gandalf seemed so freakishly tall in *The Lord of the Rings.* When done correctly, it can powerfully convey the size of a character or object within the frame without relying on CGI.

Foreground. An object or subject closest to the camera, as it is distinguished from the background.

Foreign Film. In the US, it refers to any motion picture produced outside the US and Canada, in a non-English language, and usually with funding from a non-US or Canadian source. This distinction is the basis for the award category of the same name at the Academy Awards.

Foreign Rights. The rights sold to a distributor to market, sell, and distribute the film in specific territories outside the US and Canada.

Foreshadowing. A literary device which suggests – to varying degrees of subtlety — what may happen later in the story. Foreshadowing can take many forms, such as a character's words or actions, the use of symbols or imagery, or even the tone and mood of a scene. It's like winking at your audience and saying, "Just you wait."

Format. (1) The language in which a video file is encoded onto a file. (2) The film's aspect ratio.

Fourth Wall. The invisible boundary between the fictional world and the real-life audience watching it. "Breaking the fourth wall" refers to an actor acknowledging the audience, discreetly (*Death Proof*) or indiscreetly (*Ferris Bueller's Day Off*).

Frame Rate, Frames Per Second, FPS. The frequency at which individual frames (still images) are presented to produce the illusion of motion. Most feature films should be shot and exhibited at 24 FPS (ideally!)

Frame. The individual image used in a sequence of frames or a strip of film.

Framing. The way a camera is positioned to compose a shot, and the way in which subjects and objects are positioned within the boundaries of said frame. It's one of those things that separate average film directors from amazing ones.

Franchise. A series of films that share a common core element, such as continuous characters, plot points, and themes. Most often surround a single hero or group of heroes, moving the main characters or the overall plot forward until a conclusion is reached. Examples include *Lord of the Rings*, *Star Wars*, *Harry Potter*, and *Pirates of the Caribbean*.

Freeze Frame. A single frame that stops the action and allows a frozen image to be viewed for an extended period of time, ideally accompanied by Tony Bennet's *Rags to Riches*.

French Flag, Lens Shade. A clamp flag used to shade the lens and prevent undesired flare.

Frequency, Frequency Response. The measurement of output sensitivity in both sound recording systems and video playback.

Frequency. The number of times a signal vibrates every second, measured in Hertz (Hz).

Fresnel Lens. A stepped-convex lens consisting of many small pieces of glass that allow large apertures and short focal lengths. Fresnel lenses are commonly used in lighting and projection systems, where they focus and control the direction of light.

Fringes. In film budgeting, an additional hiring cost such as payroll taxes, health care, pension plans, etc.

Fringing, Chromatic Aberration, Color Fringing. A type of distortion that keeps the lens from focusing color accurately. The result is color bleeding along boundaries that separate dark and bright parts of the image. A common issue with cheap lenses.

Front Projection. A process of shooting actors and foreground objects in front of a pre-shot projection, common in Hitchcock movies and driving scenes shot before cameras were easily rigged onto cars.

FUI. In film budgeting, FUI stands for Federal Unemployment Insurance. Typically found in the budget under the Fringes category. You have to pay for it, it's the freaking law!

Full Coat. A film layer on which sound is recorded and from which it is reproduced.

Full Tarantino. A humorous expression, going "Full Tarantino" refers to the filming of an especially bloody scene, alluding, of course, to master filmmaker Quentin Tarantino's penchant for graphic violence.

Furnie Blanket, Furni Pad. A special blanket used to protect equipment, props, locations, and everything else that might get damaged during filming. If you have to lay down and rest on a set, don't sleep on it, it doesn't smell great.

FX. Abbreviation for Effects. In the same family as SFX (Practical Special Effects), VFX (Visual Effects) and Sound SFX (Special Sound Effects).

G

G. The MPAA rating designated to inform audiences that a film is suitable for viewing by all audiences, with minimal depictions of violence and no nudity, sex scenes, or drug use - so none of the fun stuff basically.

Gaffer Tape, Gaff, Gaff Tape. A type of cloth or electrical tape used primarily by the electricians on film shoots. Gaffer tape is stronger than duct tape and does not leave a sticky residue - something we can all agree is good to have.

Gaffer, Chief Lighting Technician. The head electrician, responsible for the design and execution of the lighting plan for a film shoot.

Gain. An increase in audio signal amplification. Expressed in decibels (db).

Gamma. The level of contrast in an image as captured by a camera and corrected to compensate for properties of human vision.

Gamut. (1) The limited range of colors available in a device or file format. (2) The range of allowable voltage for a video signal.

Gang Boss. A menacing name for the person in charge of a construction crew.

Gang Synchronizer. A device used to synchronize film and audio tracks recorded on magnetic film.

Garbage Matte. A digital tool for removing undesired chroma residue ignored by a green-screen or blue-screen key effect. It helps clean up a green screen shot.

Gary Coleman. An offensive term for a small C-stand or short tripod.

Gate. The little window in film cameras through which the film is exposed to light. Whenever you hear someone yell, "Check the gate!" it's to ensure that the gate is free of hairs, dirt, or any other blockages that might ruin the shot. "Gate is clean" means you're good to go and move on to the next shot.

Gauge. The width of a film format, measured in millimeters (35mm, 16mm, etc.)

Gel. (1) A tinted, transparent sheet placed over a light source to add or change color. (2) That thing you put in your hair on the last day of shooting, because you want to make a good last impression!

Gender Twist, Gender-Bending. When a character is played by an actor of the opposite sex. Examples include Julie Andrews in *Victor Victoria*, Dustin Hoffman in *Tootsie*, and Rob Schneider in *The Hot Chick*.

General Release. The release of a film to the public via theaters, DVD, subscription, on-demand, etc..

Generator, Genie. An engine which generates electricity; a useful tool for when shooting on location and electricity is not available, or for when you need a little more juice and the location is so old you fear the walls might collapse if you plug an extra curling iron in.

Genie Operator, or Genie Op. The member of the crew who operates the generator. That thing we mentioned a second ago.

Genlock. A device used to synchronize multiple cameras or other video sources together, as well as synchronize audio and video signals, saving you time in post.

Genre. A grouping or classification of films that share similar themes, settings, plot elements, and visual style. Genres help filmmakers and studios target specific audiences, they also help viewers decide what type of movie they want to watch. Film genres can include drama, comedy, action, horror, fantasy, romance, sci-fi, and many others. Genre also encapsulates sub-genres, which are more specific categories within larger film genres. Examples include neo-noir, romantic comedy, slasher horror, space opera, the list goes on.

Gigabyte (GB). A unit for measuring a computer's memory capacity. 1GB is the equivalent of 1,000MB or, megabytes. It's that thing you want a million of, but can only afford a few hundred of.

Gimbal. A digital device that allows the camera to capture stable, smooth shots in a similar fashion to a Steadicam. It works about half the time, but when it does - it yields worthwhile results.

Giraffe. A stand and a boom-pole in one.

Globes. A type of light bulb used to produce a warm color temperature, making your scene feel all warm and fuzzy.

Go For. A radio call for a specific person on set, e.g., "Go for Mr. Gibson."

Gobo Head, Grip Head. A useful mount that offers a firm hold on rods with diameters of 5/8" and 3/8". Its ability to provide precise positioning of nets, flags, lights, and props make it an essential tool for productions.

Gobo, Goes Before Optics. A versatile and essential tool used to control and manipulate light. It is typically a small metal or glass disc that is placed inside or in front of a lighting fixture to create a shape or pattern of light and shadow.

Gobo Arm. An adjustable clamp mounted at the top of a C-Stand.

Gofer. Short for "go for." A production assistant or intern hired to handle any task involving running, driving, walking, or crawling somewhere to pick up or deliver stuff to people (scripts, lunch, coffee, discrete bottles of alcohol, etc.)

Grading. The post-production process of altering or enhancing the overall look of a shot or scene by adjusting its colors, saturation and contrast. Color grading is used to help establish a mood by manipulating colors, it's a crucial part of the finishing process in post-production, and it's the thing that amateur filmmakers always get wrong when they flood the shot with a blue contrasty tint, because "that's how Nolan does it."

Graphic Artist. An artist who designs the graphic elements that appear on-screen. In addition to the design and typography for opening credits, a graphic designer creates all the signs and other graphics on the outside and inside of buildings and objects in the film. In other words, they really have Photoshop down to a science.

Greek. To modify the name of a product on a package to avoid copyright or trademark infringement issues. This could be done on set or in post.

Green Screen Compositing. The post-production process of removing green or blue elements from a shot and replacing them with another image. This is a common method used to replace backgrounds and make it look like your scene is taking place in a country that you can't afford to fly to.

Green Screen. A green cloth or wall used for green screen compositing, duh.

Greenlight. The official studio approval of a film that has been in development's budget, meaning it's ready to go into production!

Greens. Any vegetation that is procured, placed, and maintained on a set.

Greensman. A member of the crew responsible for arranging and maintaining landscape vegetation on set. They're the ones you want to have around when the time comes to create a scene in the suburbs, the woods, or a prehistoric forest.

Grifflon, Griff. A durable surface used to reflect and bounce light. Not to be confused with Gryffindor, the house we all want to be in despite knowing that we'll never get in,

Grindhouse, Action House. A name used to describe a movie theater specializing in screening violent, exploitative, or X-rated low budget films. Grindhouse films were produced specifically for such theaters. Examples include *Coffy, Master of the Flying Guillotine, The Texas Chainsaw Massacre, Rolling Thunder*, and *Death Proof*.

Grip 10. A 10-ton truck used to transport grip equipment. It's big, heavy, and you're not allowed to drive it.

Grip Clips. A handy clip used to attach some things to other things around the set.

Grip Tape. Another name for Gaffer Tape.

Grip. Skilled lighting and rigging technician responsible for maintaining and operating production equipment such as tripods, dollies, tracks, cranes, etc.

Gross Participation. A contractual agreement in which the director or a star is guaranteed a specific percentage of a film's gross proceeds, the 'first dollar', or money that a film takes in before the cost of making it is deducted. It is sometimes used when a major star agrees to receive a lower paycheck in exchange for 'back-end' or gross participation. It's what every low budget indie film promises to a big star before being told by their agent that they're too busy to read your script.

Gross. The total sum of box-office revenue generated by the film before the studio deducts their "expenses", which includes production costs, salaries, limos, strip clubs, and various other legitimate expenses.

Guerilla Film. A very low-budget film, typically shot without permits with a minimal, often unpaid cast and crew. Famous examples include *El Mariach, Paranormal Activity, Following,* and *The Blair Witch Project.*

Guillotine Splicer. Slang for a film splicer.

Guilty Pleasure Film. A film enjoyed regardless of its public reception or negative reviews. Often cheesy or badly acted films; so bad it's good! Famous examples include *The Toxic Avenger, Garbage Pail Kids Movie, Road House,* and *Tango and Cash.*

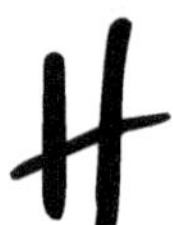

Hair Department. Where bad hair days come to die. The hair department is responsible for taming, snipping, and styling hair, wigs, and even beards on set. Without it, we'd have a whole lot of unruly locks and patchy facial hair on screen.

Hair Department Head, Key Hair. A key department head is in charge of their specific department, the hair department is no exception. They work closely with the director, cinematographer, costume designer, and makeup department head to make sure the actors' hairstyles are cohesive with the film's aesthetic. They're also responsible for managing the department's budget, supplies, scheduling, and test days.

Hair Stylists. The trained technicians responsible for styling and maintaining the hair of the actors on set. They play a crucial role in bringing characters to life on screen by creating hairstyles that are visually striking, authentic, and contribute to the overall storytelling.

Handheld Shot. A shooting style in which a camera is manually held by the operator or is placed on his/her shoulder, as opposed to placing it on a tripod, dolly or crane. Some filmmakers avoid it, some overuse it, and some *know* how to use it. Watch Spielberg, he gets it.

Handle. In editing, a handle is extra material added to both ends of a print to use for transitions. The same principle applies to VFX shots and digital footage. Because more is almost always, more… and rarely a waste.

Hard Disk. A data storage medium, or as you might refer to it - a hard drive.

Hard Drive. See, Hard Disk.

Hardware Calibration. The method of adjusting color, highlights, or darks in a monitor with a device such as a digital camera.

Hays Code, The Motion Picture Production Code of 1930. A set of rules about what was allowed or not allowed to be seen on-screen. In short, the Hays Code censored the f**k out of everything (see what we did there?). By the late 1960s, enforcement of the code had become next to impossible and the Production Code was abandoned entirely.

Haze! A call to activate the smoke machine or haze machine. Ideally called *before* you start rolling, so that you don't just sit and wait around for the haze to (slowwwly) fill the space as everyone on set twiddles their thumbs in awkward silence.

Hazeltine. A color-timing machine which determines how to 'time' a film print for the proper amounts of red, blue, and green light.

HDMI. High Definition Multimedia Interface used for transmitting HD Digital Audio and video data. In other words, it's an HD video cable, that thing you plug into the back of your TV.

Head Carpenter. A key member of the construction department, responsible for overseeing the building, rigging, and striking of all sets and scenic elements. They're the ones who make sure all the sets are built on time, on budget, and without falling apart (unless it's part of the script!).

Head-On Shot. When objects or subjects are moving directly towards the camera.

Head. (1) The beginning of a shot or a roll. (2) The Tripod Head. (3) The department head. (3) That thing you'd lose if it wasn't attached.

Headroom. The space between the top of a character's head and the top of the frame. The bigger the actor's head, the further away you have to be with the camera.

Heat Resistant Gloves. Heat-resistant leather gloves that provide secure use during various rigging. Especially helpful when touching lights, those suckers get HOT!

Helicopter Shot. An aerial moving shot; shot from a helicopter, typically.

Helm or Helmer. The film's director, the person in charge of pretty much everything.

Hero, Heroine. The film's principal character; the protagonist.

Hertz, Hz. A unit of measurement used to measure the frequency of musical tones.

Hi Hat. A square plywood tripod-head-mount used for ground shots or low shots, something you wish you had when the time comes to get down and dirty with a character on the floor.

Hi-Con. A high-contrast film print.

High-Boy, Overhead Stand. A heavy-duty, rolling stand, used primarily for lighting set-ups.

High Concept. Stories that can be easily described and marketed based on a simple and easily recognizable premise or idea. They typically involve a unique and attention-grabbing concept that can be communicated quickly and effectively to potential audiences. Examples include *Groundhog Day*, *Ghostbusters*, *Speed*, and the ultimate Christmas movie, *Die Hard*.

High Definition, HD, High-Def. A general term used to describe a video signal with a resolution higher than that of Standard Definition. Additionally, HD footage is commonly shot on a wider aspect ratio than that of Standard Definition.

High key. A well-lit scene noted by the absence of shadows, popular in sitcoms, romantic comedies, and that movie you tried to DP yourself.

High-Angle Shot. When a shot is filmed from above, generally with the use of a crane or drone.

High-Pass Filter. An electronic audio filter used to reduce all frequencies below a chosen frequency.

Highlighting. The use of light beams to illuminate a selected feature of the subject (like the eyes), while keeping the rest of the subject hidden in shadow.

Hiss. A background noise caused by imperfections in the recording medium; designed to remind you of your mortality - because *perfect* doesn't exist, apparently.

Histogram. A visual representation of data, charting exposure values along a bar graph from dark to bright.

Hitchcockian. A scene, film, or sequence containing visual or story elements similar to those of Alfred Hitchcock.

Hitting a Mark. The specific landing spot, or "mark" that an actor needs to arrive at through their blocking so that they can be filmed or seen clearly and effectively by the camera. Just in case you thought acting was an easy job… it's not.

HMI, Halogen Metal Incandescent Light. A very heavy, large, bright, and powerful light designed to illuminate things, preferably big things.

HOD. Abbreviation for the Head of the Department.

Hold for Sound! Uttered, whispered, or screamed by a sound recorder or boom operator when an unwanted sound suddenly occurs and threatens to ruin a take.

Hold. (1) Used in continuity reports to indicate that a particular take should be kept, but not developed. (2) Uttered on set by a department head just before the camera rolls when something quick needs fixing. Everyone stop what you're doing so we can fix this and move on with our day, please!

Hollywood Box. A stage plug-type box without fuses.

Hollywood-It, to "Hollywood" Something. A colloquialism to request to simply hand-hold a piece of grip equipment or a light, instead of setting it up on a C-stand. Useful when walking with actors or when the AD is screaming in your ear that you're running out of time!

Homage, Pay Homage. A film or scene that includes elements that imitate (in a respectful fashion) the work of a master, influential director. Because it's not stealing, it's homage!

Honeywagon. A celebrity, star, production, makeup, portable toilets, or wardrobe trailer. Sometimes it's a luxury, other times - a must!

Hoofer. A somewhat archaic term for a dancer, particularly a show dancer or chorus dancer.

Horror. One of the oldest genres in the film book, horror films aim to scare the bejesus out of you by using all sorts of frightening elements, from monsters to ghosts, to chainsaw-wielding psychos. They're not just about jump scares and gore, though - horror films can explore deeper themes like mortality, the unknown, and psychological trauma. There are tons of sub-genres within horror such as slashers, supernatural, monster movies, etc. Horror films have been around for over a century, drawing inspiration from folklore, superstitions, and Gothic literature.

Horse Opera. Slang for a Western. A genre of movies that typically features cowboys, gunslingers, rugged landscapes, and…horses.

Hot Brick. A fully charged walkie-talkie battery.

Hot Light. A light source level of brightness that causes overexposure. "Too hot" means that a light source is too bright and needs to be dimmed down, unless you want your shot to burn out. #YouDoYou

Hot Mic. An active microphone, sometimes referred to when someone speaks without realizing their mic is on.

Hot Points. Called when carrying something big, heavy, or hot.

Hot, Prop. A prop that has been checked and prepared for use in a scene, typically referring to a prop gun. A hot gun is ready to fire, a hot car is ready to drive.

Hot Set. A particular area of the set that is ready for filming and should not be disturbed. A hot set sign is typically put up to ensure that everything remains in place for the sake of continuity.

Hot Shoe. A small mount used to support external microphones, electronic viewfinders, and field monitors. If you ever want to mount a mic on top of your camera, a hot shoe is your friend.

Hot Splicer. An electric cement splicer for film.

House Sync. An internal timing signal used to sync devices within a facility.

Housekeeping Deal. When a film studio gives a writer, producer, director, or leading actor an office space on the lot in return for the rights of first refusal to distribute his or her upcoming projects. It's that thing you get when you know you're hot stuff!

Hue. The attribute of a color.

Hybrid Film. A film combining multiple genres, styles, or formats to create a unique cinematic experience. These films may combine live-action footage with animation, or blend genres such as comedy and drama. The goal of a hybrid film is to create something new and innovative by breaking the traditional boundaries of film-making. Examples of hybrid films include *Who Framed Roger Rabbit* (Animation/Live Action), *Cowboys & Aliens* (Western/Sci-Fi), and *Pickings* (Neo-Noir/Spaghetti Western).

Hype, Hyperbole. Overzealous praise or advertising to create buzz and excitement about a project that doesn't necessarily turn out to merit the attention or claims that were made. Not to be confused with "buzz", which is created organically.

Hyperfocal Distance. A distance set on the focus ring of the lens beyond which all objects can be brought into an "acceptable" focus.

I

IATSE. The International Alliance of Theatrical Stage Employees. It's the "go to" North American labor union, representing over 150,000 technicians, artisans, and craftspersons in the entertainment industry.

Iconography. Recognizable visual symbols used to convey key information about a story, genre or timeframe. For example, Western Iconography includes ten-gallon hats, spurs, horses, saloons, and squinting men in loosely-fitted leather pants.

Illegal Colors. Colors used in a video file which are not supported by the video playback system, causing the monitor to panic and dial 911.

Illustrator. An artist responsible for designing and drawing characters, shots, scenes and any other visual representations needed by and under the supervision of the director or the production designer. Sometimes credited as Concept Artists.

Image Stabilization. An automatic, in-camera function to reduce shakiness and make the shot appear smoother. It's like having a personal steadicam operator on set, minus the cost and the need for a human to carry it.

IMAX. Widescreen technology that produces an image approximately ten times greater than the images reproduced on standard 35mm film (up to 18K). Because you need to pay extra for that level of immersion if you're going to sit through two hours of *Ant-Man and the Wasp: Quantumania*.

IMDB, IMDBPro. An internet database in which filmmaking professionals are listed along with their credits, current projects and representation or other contact information.

In point. The edit-point at which a clip begins. Opposite of end point.

In-Camera Editing. The amateur process of shooting scenes in the exact order in which they will appear because the filmmaker can't afford an editor and thinks Premiere is a microwave brand.

Incident Light Reading. Using a light-meter to measure the amount of light as it shines on or hits a subject or object.

Incoming Scene. The second scene in a transition.

Independent Film, Indie, Indie Film. A film produced outside of the major film studio system, typically at a lower budget tier. What indie films lack in budget, they make up for in creative freedom and experimental storytelling. Indie filmmakers have the power to take risks and explore unique themes. These films don't always have the luxury of a big marketing budget, so they often rely on non-traditional distribution channels like film festivals, art-house theaters, and online streaming platforms; they are often financed through private investors, crowdfunding campaigns, or personal funds. Examples include *Get Out* (2017), *Whiplash* (2014), *Blue Ruin* (2013), and *Juno* (2007) to name a few.

Independent Spirit Awards, Spirit Awards. The annual awards and ceremony honoring achievements in indie film. The cooler version of the Oscars.

Indie Filmmaker. From writing the screenplay to directing, producing, and editing the final product, indie filmmakers are the ultimate jack-of-all-trades. They make their movies *independently*, outside of the traditional studio system, with lower budgets, smaller crews, and without the involvement (or financial backing) of major film studios. They're known for their creative freedom and willingness to take risks in storytelling and filmmaking techniques, as well as their exploration of unconventional themes and stories that might not otherwise be seen on the big screen.

IndieClear. A company that specializes in script clearance research reports for independent film, television, new media, and web productions. They're awesome! And no, I was not paid to write that (yet!).

Infinity. The furthest possible distance on the focus ring– it's where bokeh goes to die.

Ingenue. (1) A young and innocent female character, e.g.; Agatha in *The Grand Budapest Hotel*, Cecile Caldwell in *Cruel Intentions* or Jovie in *Elf*. (2) A young actress who is in the early stage of her career and whose youthful appearance is suited to such film roles.

Inkie. A small, fresnel type light. It sounds so darn cute!

Inks, Inked. A colloquial expression used to mean that someone has signed the contract, the deal is now written in ink and thus, fully official. Let the legally ambiguous, yet threatening emails begin!

Inning. A period of time within a larger event, similar to an inning in baseball.

Insert Edit. Inserting and/or replacing a clip into a timeline.

Insert Shot. A shot of an object relevant to the on-screen action. For instance, a close-up shot of a lighter flame might be inserted during a medium shot of a person lighting a cigarette. Those inserts can save your life in editing, get them while you can!

INT, Interior. A notation used in screenplays to indicate that the following scene takes place in an interior setting, or in other words… indoors.

Intellectual Property, IP. An idea, concept or story for a film that has a clear origin or creator, and which may necessitate permission to use as a basis of inspiration for a film. It's that thing you think you should have over that idea you once had, but you're not sure because you never copyrighted it!

Intended Ratio, Original Aspect Ratio. The original aspect ratio planned by the DP, often referred to because "someone" changed their minds in the edit room.

Intercut, Intercutting. An editing technique in which an editor cuts back and forth between two scenes to create the sense that the actions in these scenes are occurring simultaneously. A famous example includes the bell ring scene in *Silence of the Lambs* (1991).

Interlace Scan. The opposite of a Progressive Scan. Interlace is a technique for doubling the perceived frame rate of a video display without consuming extra bandwidth.

Interlock. When one or more machines are running in sync.

Interlude. A short, self-contained shot unrelated to the plot or sequence. Interludes can take many forms, including musical sequences, montage sequences, or brief scenes that provide context or backstory to the main narrative. They can also serve as a way to transition between different locations or time periods in the story. Not to be confused with an intermission, or a cutaway of a cat on the window.

Internegative. A duplicate color negative made from a positive print.

Interpolation. A method used in animation for automatically calculating the motion between two set keyframes, so that it is not necessary to animate each frame manually.

Interpositive. Any positive duplicate of a film that is used for additional processing.

Intertitle. A single title card that occupies the entire screen. Commonly used in silent films to relay information (often dialogue). Because we all want to know what words Chaplin characters used to pick up women.

Intervalometer. An external, unattached device used in time-lapse shots.

Intimacy Coordinator. This crewmember is responsible for making sure that on-screen sex stays safe and sane. They're like a mix of a coach, a therapist, and a referee; they ensure that the actors are following the agreed upon activity (consent is sexy), that everyone feels safe, that no one gets hurt, and that the well-being of the actors who partake in steamy sex scenes is maintained.

Into Frame. A subject or object moving into the frame during a static shot. Hopefully on purpose. Looking at you boom ops!

Investor. The beautiful person responsible for partially or fully funding a film. Investors are typically credited as Executive Producers and are the most coveted human beings in Planet Hollywood.

Invisible Cut. A fast cut made during on-camera motion that can be used to replace and match the shot seamlessly, with the result that the cut is invisible.

Iris Out, Iris Wipe. The effect of ending a shot with a closing iris circle. Commonly used in Star Wars and old Looney Tunes cartoons.

Iris. A variable aperture used to control the amount of light that passes through the lens. Most lenses have either manual or automatic iris control. Fun fact - the human eye has an iris too, but you knew that already.

ISO. An in-camera exposure sensitivity setting, like an in-camera cheat code that makes your shot brighter when all else fails. When you've cranked open your aperture and thrown every light you can afford at the scene, but it's still not bright enough, try pumping up the ISO. But keep in mind, the more ISO you add, the more noise you'll get. And the angrier your director will be at the shot.

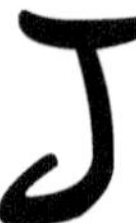

J-Lar. A transparent tape used to splice gels.

Jam Sync. The process of synchronizing time-codes between two devices.

Jell. A color gel or filter used to color light for the purpose of creating a colored lighting effect. For those times you want a blue lightning flash, or a red warning countdown to the end of the earth - Jells got your back!

Jib Arm. A mounted, counterweighted support arm used on a camera crane, designed to give the camera a wider range of motion; perfect for those overhead rainy shots where the character spins around like Tim Robbins in *The Shawshank Redemption* (1994) or Drew Barrymore in real life.

Jog. To scroll incrementally through a video by playing it one frame at a time. Not to be confused with that thing you do on the treadmill when life's got you down and your screenplay is stuck on "fade in".

Judder. The unstable motion caused by an improper frame rate conversion; it's not fun to look at.

Juice. Slang term for electricity, also you drink it.

Juicer, Sparks. Some fun slang terms for the electricians on set, just in case you wanted to know that.

Jump Cut. An abrupt camera cut intended to communicate the passing of time.

Junior. A 2K light unit.

Juxtaposition. The side-by-side positioning of two images, characters, objects, or scenes. Often used in film to produce a subliminal or philosophical effect. Just ask David Mamet, he'll tell you all about it.

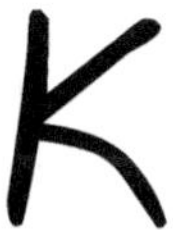

Kelvin, K. A unit of measurement for color temperature. The Kelvin temperature scale ranges from warm, yellowish light (around 2000K) to cool, bluish light (up to 10000K or more). The lower the number, the warmer and more yellowish the light appears, while higher numbers are associated with cooler and bluer tones. For example, a warm, yellowish light (around 2700K) might be used for a cozy interior scene by the fireplace, while a cooler, bluer light (around 5600K) might be used for a "running from a serial killer" outdoor night scene to create a more unsettling feel.

KEM. A well-known and commonly used flatbed film editing unit.

Key Costumer. The crew member responsible for supervising all on-set wardrobe needs and requirements, as well as the monitoring of costume continuity, ensuring that every detail of the costume remains consistent throughout filming, especially if scenes are shot out of order. Can you imagine if a character's shirt magically changed colors halfway through the shot? Well, hire a key costumer, and you won't have to!

Key Frame. A frame that marks the starting and end points of a transition.

Key Grip. The head of the grip department, they are responsible for providing support to the gaffer, the camera, and lighting departments by setting up camera and lighting rigs, as well as hiring and supervising the grip crew. They're like the MacGyvers of the movie world, always ready with a grip clip and some gaff tape to make your day a little easier.

Key Hair. The Hair Department chief responsible for designing and styling the hair of the lead actors, making sure your character has a good hair day (or a particularly bad one).

Key Light. The primary light source that sets the tone for your entire scene. Its strength, color, and angle all play a major role in determining how your shot will look.

Key Makeup, Makeup Head. Makeup department head who plans, designs, and executes makeup for all leading and supporting cast. This person is in charge of making sure the actors look their best (or worst, depending on the scene). They typically manage a team of makeup artists and ensure that the makeup design and application are consistent with the overall creative vision for the film, as well as keeping the budget intact.

Key Numbers. A series of unique identification numbers embedded at the edge of film stock by the manufacturer.

Key Scenic. A crew member responsible for surface looks and treatments on set, such as special paints and textures. They typically supervise the painting crew and produce the realistic looks needed for the miniatures.

Keyframe Animation. A marked frame containing animation information.

Keying. A term for removing green-screen / blue-screen information (chroma key) from an image.

Keykode. A machine developed by Kodak to automate the creation of film cut lists.

Kick-Off. The official start of principal photography.

Kick. An object receiving a shine or bounced light.

Kill. The commonly used, slang term for turning something off, e.g., "kill the lights". Also, murder.

Kinoflo, Kino Flo. A lighting manufacturer that develops and manufactures Lightbank kits.

Kiss. A soft light that illuminates a subject or object gently.

Klieglight. A powerful carbon-arc lamp capable of shining intense light.

L-cut, Split Cut. A cut made in the editing of digital film in which the audio starts before or after the picture. In other words, you might hear a character's voice before you see their face, or vice versa. This creates a sense of anticipation and suspense, and can be used to draw the viewer's attention to a particular aspect of the scene.

L.C.R.S (Left, Center, Right, Surround). The original Dolby Pro Logic format was released before the 5.1 Surround Format, which is now more commonly used.

Lamp. The bulb inside a lighting unit, also - it gives light!

Landmark Film. A revolutionary film recognized by and included in the National Film Registry; typically the subject of obsession and discussion amongst film students, professors, and that friend of yours who won't stop talking about *The Godfather*. Landmarked films include such titles as *Pulp Fiction* (1994), *Citizen Kane* (1941), and *The Godfather* (1972).

Lap, Lap Dissolve. A shot in which one image gradually transitions – or dissolves – into the next image, with the first image already fading by the time the next one can be seen.

Last Looks, Final Looks. A call to a department to check a subject or set before the camera rolls. Often used to check an actor's makeup or hair; so if you're looking at the monitor and sees an untreated zit on an unsuspecting actor's face, call it out "last looks!", the actor will love you.

Latitude. The range of exposure that a film or digital camera sensor can capture while still retaining detail in both the brightest and darkest areas of the image. It is often used to describe a camera's ability to capture a wide range of contrast and detail in a scene.

Lavalier, Lavalier Mic, Lavalier Microphone, Lav. A small wireless microphone that can easily be hidden in clothing. Lavalier mics come in both wired and wireless versions, connected directly to a recording device or sound system via a cable, or via a radio frequency or infrared signals.

Layback. The process of transferring a completed sound mix back onto the video master tape.

Layoff. The transfer of audio and timecode from the video edit master to an audio tape.

Layout Artist. A post-production artist responsible for staging VFX shots and assisting the director with planning the framing of on-screen plates.

Layouts. The plans for the framing in a VFX or animation shot. Layouts are all about planning the framing of each shot to achieve a visual effect, figuring out where the camera should be placed and how the scene should be framed.

Figuring out where the characters will be positioned, and what the overall mood of the shot will be. Not to be confused with Storyboarding.

Layover. The transfer of audio to a multi-track tape or hard disk.

Lead Character Technical Director. A VFX artist responsible for the development of characters, creatures, and mechanical objects. The role of a character TD may vary in its scope depending on the studio, but typically centers around the process of character rigging (The process of creating a digital skeleton to control movement and animation of a CG model.)

Lead, Leading Actor. An actor who plays the primary or central character in a film. Often the most prominent character in the story and is typically given the most screen time, lines, and character development. They are responsible for carrying the emotional weight of the story and driving the plot forward. Talk about being your favorite child!

Leader. A length of material added to the beginning or end of each reel, used for identification, or fill-in purposes.

Leadman. A set decoration department member responsible for the props and swing gang and/or the set dressers on a film set.

Legal Color Limiting. A method of clipping electronic signals to conform to the minimum and maximum levels permitted for use in broadcast television.

Legal Counsel, Legal Services. The production's entertainment lawyer, responsible for negotiating contracts, clearing licensing rights, obtaining tax credits, and making sure you don't get sued into oblivion!

Legal Signal. A signal that must not exceed the specified gamut for the current format.

Leko. An ellipsoidal reflector spotlight.

Lens Flare. An optical phenomenon that occurs when a bright light source shines directly into the lens of a camera. While it is generally considered to be a detracting factor in image quality, there are instances where it can be intentionally used to enhance the visual appeal of the picture. Just ask J. J. Abrams - he'll tell you all about it.

Lens Hood, Lens Shade. A doodad used on the front end of a lens to block the sun or other unwanted light sources in order to prevent glare and lens flare.

Lens Mount. An opening on a camera that is designed to securely attach and hold a lens in place. It is a physical interface that connects the camera body and the lens, allowing them to communicate with each other. Different camera brands and models often have different types of lens mounts, which are designed to work with specific lenses.

Lens Res. Short for Lens Resolution; an indicator of how much detail a lens can capture without diminishing the quality of said detail.

Lens. A piece of optical equipment that is designed to focus light onto a camera's image sensor or film to create beautiful images that make our hearts sing and our emotions flare up at the sight of Emma Stone and Ryan Gosling. Lenses come in a variety of focal lengths and apertures, and they can be interchangeable or permanently fixed to the camera body. Camera lenses can also have a range of features, such as zoom, image stabilization, and autofocus. The quality of a camera lens is a critical factor in determining the quality of the final image, and high-quality lenses can produce sharper, clearer, and more detailed images than lower-quality ones.

Let's Roll! A request to pick up the pace and move more quickly — aka the AD is freaking out and wants to get this show on the road!

Letterboxing. The process of placing black bars at the top and bottom of a standard definition image to make it look like a Widescreen image. The "poor man's" widescreen, as the folks who can afford widescreen cameras call it.

Level. A measurement of amplitude in decibels.

Lexan. A flame retardant sheet used to protect crew from explosions or fire effects., because catching on fire is no picnic.

Libra Head. A digitally stabilized 3 axis remote head.

Library Shot. Another term for stock footage.

Light Gags. A light that is used to produce a particular special effect, such as a TV or fireplace flicker, police lights, or whatever was coming out of ET's finger.

Light Meter. A device used to measure the amount of light in a given space. Often used by DPs and gaffers to determine the proper exposure for a shot.

Light Value. A fast-opening shutter controlling the light intensity in printing film.

Lighting Board Operator, Light Op. A crew member responsible for controlling the level or intensity of on-set lights. In some cases, the light op may also serve as the film's lighting designer. They're responsibilities include creating a lighting plot, hanging and focusing lighting instruments, and programming complex lighting cues involving multiple fixtures and components.

Lighting Crew. Another term for Gaffers; lighting crew consists of the technicians responsible for installing, operating, and maintaining the lights on set and on location.

Lighting Department. The department responsible for designing, procuring, setting up, and running the lights on a shoot. Stuff gets hot, real fast, so better bring your gloves.

Lighting Technician. A crew member responsible for setting up and controlling lighting equipment on set. They help create the desired atmosphere for the scene and make sure that the scene is as bright (or dark) as needed. They assemble and test lighting equipment, organize scaffolding and cranes, pre-rig lighting, check the focus of lighting, operate and maintain equipment during shoots, program and operate lighting consoles, and dismantle and store equipment safely.

Lighting. The manipulation of light and shadows to compose a visually appealing shot, there are no movies (or life) without it.

Light leak. When a light penetrates through a hole or gap in the body of a camera, leaking onto the lens and ruining (or saving) your shot.

Line Producer, LP. A film producer responsible for pretty much everything from managing the budget to overseeing operations from start to finish. They work closely with the executive producer, producer, and other department heads to create a preliminary budget and a meticulous shooting schedule. They're the ones who keep the wheels turning, so that you can make your B movie monster masterpiece.

Line! A request by an actor who forgot his lines to have them be read out loud.

Linear Editing. An outdated form of video editing in which the editor selects, arranges and modifies shots in a predetermined sequence.

Lined Script. A shooting script that includes shot and coverage information.

Lines. Dialogue spoken by the characters in a script.

Lip Sync. The synchronization of mouth movements (image) with recorded audio (sound). So… it's pretty important.

Liquid Gate, Wet-transfer. A film printing system used to reduce visible surface scratches and abrasions. Commonly used for film restoration and archival scanning, because old stuff is awesome, and we must preserve it!

Live Area. The complete, unclipped area that appears in a camera's viewfinder, taking advantage of the full frame before you ruin it with your "borders."

Loading Booth. A portable dark room used for loading film into magazines, also a great place to sit in the dark between setups if you want some peace and quiet.

Loan Out. A corporation set up to "loan" an actor or director for work on a production. Directors and actors would typically set up their own LLC and "loan" themselves to other productions as opposed to being hired as salaried employees. The key benefits include expense deductions, asset protection and tax deferrals. It's what successful people do when they get successful, that and throw tantrums at craft services.

Local 600. The International Cinematographers Guild, also known as IATSE Local 600, is a union that represents camera professionals across the globe. These talented individuals work in various roles within the film and television industry, including: Director of Photography, Camera Operator, Camera Assistant (1st AC, 2nd AC), Digital Imaging Technician, Still Photographer, and all other members of camera crews. So definitely not your average "free DP with camera needed, food and credit provided" Craigslist contenders.

Location Assistant. An entry-level role within the location department. They assist the location manager with various tasks, such as leafleting, mapping, preparing movement orders, organizing on-location parking, directing pedestrian traffic, and answering questions from pesky locals and curious bystanders. Who wouldn't want to do that for 12 hours every day?

Location Manager. A crucial member of the film crew, responsible for finding and securing locations for filming, while also coordinating logistics for the production. They oversee location negotiations, preparation, wrap and strike of the location, and ensure that it is returned to its original condition. Nothing worse than screening phone calls from angry landlords screaming about cracked toilet bowls.

Location Mixer. The sound department head, responsible for capturing all sound on set during filming. This includes choosing and deploying microphones, selecting recording media, and mixing audio signals in real-time. When the budget is there, they may also be responsible for hiring the boom operator, and on low-budget shoots, they ARE the boom operator.

Location Scout. Responsible for conducting extensive research, exploring potential locations, and taking photographs to document their findings. The scout does most of the legwork required to identify suitable filming locations.

Location, Location Filming, Location Shooting. When filming on a location not specifically constructed for the production. So… anywhere outside the studio, really.

Lock It Down, Quiet on the Set. Something the director, AD, or Boom Op screams right before "speeding"; when a set needs to be cleared and kept quiet.

Locked Cut, Picture Lock. The approved and final cut of a film, ready to hit the festival circuit or movie theaters all to razzle/dazzle your audiences.

Locked Down Shot. A shot taken with the camera locked-in-place while something is happening off-screen, because when the Ronin stops working and you've all but given up hope, you can always go back to the basics.

Log. A term that can be used to refer to any list or record used to keep track of time, scene descriptions, reel numbers, etc. Also, you sit on it.

Logline. A short, introductory description of what a film is about, usually written as part of the Coverage, it ultimately lands on the film's IMDB page.

Long Lens. A camera lens in which the focal length is longer than the diagonal measure of the film. A long lens has a narrow field of view and magnifies the image, while a short lens has a wide field of view and captures more of the scene. Just in case you needed a reminder.

Long Shot, LS, Full Shot. A shot captured from a great distance– think tiny cowboy on a vast expanse, or any epic where body doubles on horses ride across the field.

Long Take. A sequence shot over a long period of time, such as one featuring a long exchange of dialogue or uninterrupted action. Think Spielberg or Alejandro González Iñárritu.

Longitudinal Timecode, LTC. Timecode recorded on a videotape's audio channels, keeping playback machines synced with a master time source.

Look Development Lead. A Visual Effects artist responsible for developing photorealism and rendering for any CGI shots, they determine which shades, textures, and digital tools will create the desired effect. They're the ones making sure your villain doesn't look like The Rock in *The Mummy Returns.*

Loop. A small magnifier useful in the editing room, also– a thing that repeats itself over and over and over and over… you get it.

Looping. (1) Another word for ADR. (2) A continuous shot or sound that runs on repeat.

Lossless. A data compression format that results in no data-loss and a generally supersized file, perfect for when you have too many hard drives and not enough footage to fill them with.

Lossy. The opposite of Lossless Compression. A compression that will result in data loss but a smaller file, just don't overdo it, or you'll end up with a pixelated mess of a shot.

Lot, The Lot. The studio's headquarters which typically includes their primary office buildings, as well as various production offices, sound stages, sets, costume shops, car garages, and cafeterias. It's where the magic is made! Some studios hold public tours including the original street scenes used in many old films.

Louma Crane. An electronic, telescoping camera crane.

Low Budget. (1) A classification of the level of production, based on its budget, as a Union Tier which stipulates pay scales. (2) A colloquial but imprecise description of a film suggesting that its production values are or will be minimal. (3) A word you utter frequently as you attempt to justify your bad decisions on set. It's hard to argue against, "Low budget, baby. Low budget."

Low Con Print. A low contrast film print.

Low Key Lighting. A high-contrast artistic lighting style using one key light to light a subject and compose a shot as opposed to the traditional Three-Point Lighting Rule. Commonly used in film noir, horror genres, and shoots that must get through 25 shots overnight and have no other choice. #BurnYourBoats

Low-Angle Shot. A shot in which the camera is positioned at a low angle, much to the disgust of your actors. Opposite of High Angle Shot.

Lowboy. A heavy-duty, rolling stand, used for lighting set-ups. It includes a stand to level it on uneven ground, for those times you want to run a dolly across a sand dune.

Lowpass Filter. An audio filter that blocks the value of frequencies above a specified threshold. It has several uses, including anti-aliasing, reconstruction, and speech processing.

LQV. A color space used to accurately represent the color and brightness of digital images. Because monitors lie!

Luma Key. Creating a matte based on the brightness data in a shot.

Luminance. A measure of brightness or intensity of pixels, the higher the brighter.

LUT. A shortcut tool that helps DP's and colorists transform color input values by using a preset "look". Can also be used as a reference point on-camera. LUTs can be used, abused, and reused over and over when color grading skills or budgets are lacking, and yield some pretty cool results (so long as you have the right LUT!).

Lyricist. A writer who writes the words for songs.

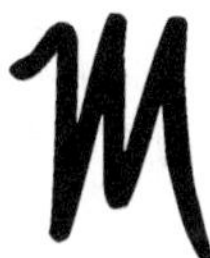

M&E Track. The abbreviation for Music and Effects. The film's soundtrack at the stage in which it contains all sounds, effects, and music — but no dialogue. An M&E track is used for foreign language dubbing. Because we all want to know what our actors sound like in a foreign language!

MacGuffin. A literary device that serves to trigger the action in a film but which, ironically, turns out to have little to do with the story. The device was used by Hitchcock, and he coined its name. In Hitchcock's own explanation, "The MacGuffin is the thing that the spies are after, but the audience doesn't care about," much like your hopes and dreams.

Macro Lens, Macro Shot. (1) A lens used for extreme close shots of a subject or object. Often used to capture very small details such as, for instance, the eye of a small insect or the details of a person's iris (2) An extreme closeup shot captured with a Macro Lens.

Madcap Comedy, Screwball Comedy. A wild, reckless, fast-paced comedy. Famous examples include *The Jerk, Caddyshack, Dumb and Dumber, Dinner for Schmucks*.

Made-Fors. The abbreviation for TV Movies, or movies made for Television, because the small screen is still a screen!

Mag, Magazine, Film Magazine. (1) A film-camera chamber that holds up to 1,000 feet of film. One camera can hold up to three magazines. (2) A RED Cinema Camera hard drive.

Magic Hour. The time of day just after sunrise or just before sunset when the light is magical and evocative. Sometimes also called the Golden Hour, the start and end times of day are filled with golden as well as pink and purplish light and can make an extraordinary backdrop for a scene.

Magnetic Film, Mag Film. A film on which sound is recorded and from which it can be reproduced.

Mainstream. A film produced for the widest audience possible - low risk, high reward, that's what this industry is all about! (evidently)

Maintenance Engineer. A crewmember responsible for general maintenance and repairs on-set; useful for when your prop computer refuses to boot.

Majors. The major Hollywood studios, Disney, Universal, Paramount, Warner Brothers.

Makeup, Makeup Artist, Make-up Supervisor. The use of cosmetics, prosthetics, and other materials to enhance or alter the appearance of actors on screen. Makeup artists work long hours to create a convincing and realistic portrayal of

a character or scene, whether it is to simulate in-
juries or aging, or to transform actors into other
beings or creatures. Film makeup can range from
subtle enhancements to extreme transformations
and will go a long way in selling the realism of a
scene. A Make-up Supervisor is responsible for
overseeing and managing the makeup department. They work closely with the director and
other departments to ensure that the makeup
design is executed accurately and on time, and
that the artists are working effectively.

Making of, The Making of. A behind-the-
scenes documentary produced by a videographer during the production of a film. With the
purpose of later use as a marketing tool for the
film, sometimes these films are added as bonus
material in the DVD release but will most often
be seen (and shared) on social media, because
that's the world we live in.

Manager. A professional who represents actors,
advising them, getting them booked on auditions, and planning their careers, all for a small
(or heavy) fee!

Mark. (1) The clapping sound made by the sticks
to sync up sound and picture in post-production.
(2) Mark Wahlberg.

Marker. Gaffer tape placed on the ground to
indicate the spot where an actor is expected to
take position, often in a menacing X shape; because you'll either hit your mark, or you're out
of focus.

Martial-Arts. The genre in which Asian combat
disciplines are featured, often Karate or Kung-
fu. Famous examples include *Fist of Fury*, *The
Grandmaster*, *Bloodsport*, and *Enter the Dragon*.

Martini Shot. The last shot of the day, after
which the cast and above the line personnel can
enjoy a nice, dirty martini in the comfort of their
trailer while the crew breaks down the set.

Mask, Masking. The process of covering-up or blocking a portion of the light, shot, object or frame either on-set or in post-production. For those happy occasions when the actor walks past a C-stand and someone needs to mask his head frame-by-frame in post.

Masking, Sound. The act of adding artificial sounds to a track for the purpose of covering up unwanted noise. So if you ever hear a loud bus go by during a line of dialogue, know that it was covering up something worse.

Massive. A high-end computer animation and artificial intelligence software used to simulate crowds. Originally invented for the *Lord of the Rings* trilogy to produce epic battle sequences.

Master Rights. A music license that allows the filmmaker to use a pre-recorded track or song in their film. Typically acquired alongside a Sync License. If you have the budget, this is once place you could spend it all!

Master Shot. A single shot — usually wide — used to capture all or most of the action in a scene, from start to finish. It captures all the characters in view from one camera angle, showing everything in one delicious take. It's typically the first shot in a new setup. Best for setting up the scene's settings, actor's blockings and position of people, lights and props within the scene.

Master, Master Print. A positive film print from which duplicate prints are processed. It's the OG print, giving birth to all the copies out there.

Match Cut. A cut made between two shots to establish the continuity of action.

Match Dissolve. A film editing technique where two shots are blended together using a transitional dissolve effect, with one shot dissolving into another shot that matches it in some way, such as color, shape, or movement. The effect creates a smooth and seamless transition between the shots.

Matchmove, Match Moving, Camera Tracking.
The process of tracking and matching the motion
of a live-action camera with that of a CGI lens, fa-
cilitating the insertion of 3D elements (dinosaurs,
spaceships, Jonah Hill) into live-action footage.

Matrix Metering. A way for a camera to divide
a wide area of the frame into multiple segments
and adjust the exposure settings precisely and
according to its meter results. Because cameras
get smarter by the year!

Matte Artist. An artist responsible for creating,
matching, and integrating matte paintings into
live action shots.

Matte Box. A square device placed in front of
the lens. Used to block sunlight and other light
while preventing glare and lens flare and allowing for the addition of various filters. It also
makes the camera look cool, so there's that!

Matte Painting. A visual effects technique that
combines hand-painted or digital artwork with
live-action footage to create the illusion of a
realistic or imaginary environment. The painted
element is often added to a scene to extend
or replace the physical set or location, creating
a larger and more detailed world. So when you
see an apocalyptic city, a vast massive landscape,
or an old castle in the distance - you'll know…
Matte paintings!

Matte Shot. The old-school version of green-
screen or blue-screen compositing. A piece of
glass was placed in front of the camera and a
strip of tape was added to obscure or alter parts
of the glass. Today, a Matte Shot is referred to as
a shot that incorporates a computerized Matte.

Maxi-Brute. A high intensity, 9Kw lighting unit
used for lighting large areas, it's the "go big or
go home" version of the light world.

MB, Megabytes. A measurement of computer
storage capability. 1MB is equal to 1,000 bytes.

MCU. (1) A medium close-up. (2) The Marvel Cinematic Universe.

Meal Penalties. A SAG term, a fine paid when the mandatory meal period is not observed by the production. In other words, better keep your cast well fed, on time, otherwise - things will not be fine! (Get it?)

Meal Periods. A SAG term referring to meal breaks, talent must be given a meal within 6 hours of first call. No pressure.

Meal. Food! Typically, a meal means a 30-minute lunch break.

Meat Axe. An arm-like clamp used by the grip department. It can pivot in all directions around the mounting clamp, allowing the G&E department to clamp flags, lights, and other accessories around the set.

MED. In film budgeting, MED stands for Medicare. Typically listed under "Fringes." It's the law, pay up!

Medium Shot. A conventional camera shot filmed from a medium distance, which presents the character or characters from the waist up.

Megaplex, Multiplex. Large movie theater complex that includes several screens or separate theaters, so that a variety of films can be shown at the same time. Famous examples include AMC, Cineworld, Cinemark and Regal.

Melodrama. A genre of dramatic films where conflicts are exaggerated and intensified, and characters shed a single tear while you go through a whole kleenex box. Examples include *Rain Man*, *City of Angels*, and *The Notebook*.

Memory Card. A portable, removable device used to store data (footage, audio) captured by digital equipment. Just make sure you format it before you bring it onto set, otherwise whatever was on it will quickly become public domain.

Mercer Clip. A small plastic clip used to hold film ends together during the assembly edit.

Merkin. A pubic wig, especially for women, placed over the public area to simulate pubic hair and shield the actor's private body parts from full exposure.

Metadata. (1) Content information related to a video file, used to inform the user of the file's settings and format. Also known as Video Metadata. (2) The distribution information related to a film, used by an aggregator to populate review sites and online resources. Also known as Distribution Metadata. They don't call it the "information age" for nothing.

Method Acting. An acting method made famous in the US by Lee Strasberg who introduced the technique for creating (in her opinion) the most realistic performance by the actor tapping into his/her emotional and sensory memories. "The Method" captivated and influenced many actors including Marlon Brando, Marilyn Monroe, Dustin Hoffman, and Robert DeNiro. In the Method, actors learn to "become the role" and may remain in character even when not in front of the camera. Not to be confused with whatever Jared Leto thinks he's doing.

Mickey. An open-faced 1K lighting unit.

Microphone Impedance. The amount of resistance a microphone has to an audio signal. A high-quality microphone has low impedance.

Microphone. Or Mic. An audio device used for capturing, converting, recording, and storing sound - there's no film without it! (unless, of course, it's a silent film).

Mighty. A 2,000-watt light fixture.

Mime. Acting without the use of words. A mime is generally restricted to the use of facial expressions, gestures and physical motions and actions.

Mini-Majors. Outside of the "Big Five," Mini-Majors are a group of smaller movie studios who do things their own way. Some of the leading mini-Majors include Lionsgate Films, MGM, Amazon Studios, Neon, A24, and STX Entertainment. They may be small, but they're mighty! And still bigger than independent studios.

Mini-Series. A television series that takes place over a set number of episodes. It was originally used to describe the 1970s newly popular format, made famous with the broadcast of *Roots*. Today, it has mostly been replaced by the term, Limited Series.

Miniature. A small-scale model used to give the illusion of a fully sized object when it is shot and manipulated through a computer. Sets for many major movies are created as miniatures including *Lord of the Rings*, *Jurassic Park*, *Star Wars*, and the *Indiana Jones* series.

Minimum Guarantee, MG. A flat fee, often paid upfront by a distributor or studio who agrees to buy the rights to distribute a film during its fundraising stages. In case you thought film financing was not complicated, MG is here to prove you wrong!

Miscast. An actor playing a role they should not be playing either because of a general lack of talent or another issue which affects the performance. Miscasted actors often get recast, which can cost the production a fortune.

Mise-en-Scene. (1) The French term used to describe everything – scenery, props, actors – set up on a stage or in front of a camera as they have been planned to appear or be filmed. (2) The factors affecting the artistic look of a shot or scene

Mix Cue Sheet. A visual aid used to locate specific sounds within a track during the mixing process.

Mix Master. The film's complete and final sound mix; typically the last step before the film is ready to be released! (are you excited yet?!)

Mix, Sound. The total sum of all combined sound (designed sound, effects, Foley, dialogue, etc.) used in a film, mastered, and blended together. Generally divided by channel.

Mixer. A crew member whose job is to mix the sound on set, maneuver the Boom Mic and keep it out of shot(!) while also making sure adequate sound is captured. On low-budget sets, the Sound Mixer doubles as a boom op... it's a rough life for folks with weak arms and weak hearing.

Mixing House. A sound studio specifically for mixing sound for film.

Mockumentary. A fictional film genre that is typically presented as a legitimate documentary, but with exaggerated or absurd elements for comedic effect. Examples of popular mockumentaries include, *This Is Spinal Tap*, *Borat*, and *What We Do in the Shadows*.

Modeler. A computer artist specializing in the creation of 3D objects — characters, buildings, vehicles, spaceships, etc. — using 3D modeling software, coffee, and a good dose of alcohol.

Modern Classic. A very popular and critically acclaimed film made in the past 10 years that is expected to become a classic in the future. These films have a high re-watch value and can be seen multiple times or revisited every year. Examples include *The Lighthouse*, *There Will be Blood*, *No Country for Old Men*, and *Pickings* - I'm fishing, I know. Shame on me.

Mogul. A popular term during the golden age of Hollywood when each studio was run by a powerful and often outsized personality. They loved publicity and were often domineering figures that included such well-known names as Louis B. Mayer (Metro Goldwyn Mayer), Jack Warner (Warner Brothers), and Carl Laemmle (Universal).

Moiré. A common artifact in digital photography that results from the interaction between the sensor and repetitive patterns or details in the scene, object, or fabric being photographed.

When the level of detail exceeds the sensor's resolution, it produces a distorted wavy pattern that can be visually distracting and undesirable. In other words, no thin-striped shirts on set!

Money Shot. A climactic, stunning shot, often an action scene, that is intended to be memorable.

Monitor. An LCD screen that the director uses during the shoot to analyze how the scene will appear on screen. Cinematographers, focus pullers, makeup artists, script supervisors and others should also have access to monitors to check the quality of the frame while it's being shot.

Monologue. A long speech by a single character.

Monopod. A single staff or pole used in lieu of a tripod to help support cameras or other gear. For those days when you film without a permit and need to get a steady shot really quick before the cops come closing in!

Montage. (1) An assembly of shots, images and brief clips put together into a sequence for the purpose of condensing information over time and place. Often used to fill in the blanks for viewers when the narrative jumps ahead over many years. (2) Any sequence of filmed images cut together to convey information visually rather than verbally, as with the In Memoriam segment during the Academy Awards.

Mood Board. A visual presentation used to convey a feeling, mood, or cinematic inspiration to a film.

Moppet. Archaic term for a child actor, replaced with "kiddo", or "kid", or literally anything else.

Morph Cut. A video transition feature that helps create a seamless shot by reducing the visibility of distracting jump cuts within the same shot. A pretty nifty little digital tool.

Morph. (1) The digital transformation and alteration of an image or a 3D model. (2) To change the look and identity of a living creature.

MOS. Acronym for Motor Out of Sync (or Mit-out Sound), used to describe a shot where no sound is being recorded. In a script, MOS is often used as an abbreviation to indicate a silent shot or scene that does not require any dialogue or sound effects.

Motif. A recurrent literary or cinematic device that involves the repetition of a narrative element that serves to support the underlying theme of a story. In film, motifs may take various forms, including physical objects, sound design, dialogue, music, colors, and symbols. Famous examples include the act of eating in *2001: A Space Odyssey* (a movie about evolution), the use of moonlight in the film *Moonlight*, The use of red balloons to signal an unseen threat to children in the Stephen King *It* films, etc.

Motion Artifact. Optical distortion caused by the motion of the object, oftentimes because of frame rate or shutter speed was set incorrectly by a soon-to-be-fired 1st AC.

Motion Blur. A visual phenomenon that occurs when a camera or its subject is in motion, resulting in streaking or smearing of the image. In real life, our eyes naturally register motion blur, so incorporating it in films helps create a more realistic portrayal of movement. Nearly all films incorporate some degree of motion blur, so long as they're shot at the conventional 24fps. This is because audiences have become conditioned to expect it in both real life and on-screen, making it a natural part of the cinematic experience. In fact, eliminating motion blur can make a film appear unnatural or artificial (looking at you two, *The Hobbit* and *Avatar: The Shape of Water!*)

Motion Builder. A 3D character animation software used to capture and transform Motion Capture data, useful for when you want your characters to move around realistically.

Motion Capture, Mocap. A method of capturing real-world actor motion (including facial motion and expression) and digitally converting it for use in a 3D application, makes the process of animating easier, faster, and cheaper.

Motion Control Technician. A technician responsible for operating motion control rigs, precision and repetition is the name of their game!

Motion Control. A way of setting up camera motions with a specialized rig for the purpose of replicating camera movement or producing complex motions that cannot be handled by an operator. It's every little DP's dream come true!

Motion Picture Association of America, MPAA. An organization that rates a film's suitability for certain audiences. They're the ones who make sure your 8 year old kid doesn't get exposed to *Hereditary* trailers during previews, or ends up in the theater during a midnight screening of *Blue is the Warmest Color*.

Motion Picture Editors Guild, MPEG. A professional advocacy affiliation, similar to a union, for qualified motion picture and sound editors.

Motion Picture, Motion Pictures. Another term for movies, cinema, films, or flicks. It's what this book is all about!

Movement Coach. A professional with experience in a variety of physical techniques who trains actors to portray the physical traits and activities of their on-screen character. In other words, actors who get paid millions of dollars to pretend to be monkeys better walk like darn monkeys!

Movie of the Week, MOW. A feature movie made expressly for TV, usually by the network itself, that is shown exclusively on the small screen. In the 1970s, ABC broadcast an original movie weekly.

Moviola. An upright film editing machine that was the go-to method for film editing through the 1970s or until flat-bed machines came into use followed by the development of software for computer editing. It was the next big thing, before being replaced by the next big thing. #Technology

MOW. Short for "Make Own Way", a cast or crew member who has their own method of transportation to get to the set for their call time.

MS. Medium shot, waist to head.

Multi-Track. More than two audio tracks.

Multichannel. Employing more than one audio channel.

Musco Lights. Powerful HMI lights mounted on a crane, because sometimes "extra" really is, "extra!"

Music Editor. A post-production artist responsible for editing the musical score.

Music Preparation. Preparation of parts of the score for the musicians to play during recording sessions.

Music Supervisor. A specialist negotiator who coordinates the sources for a movie's soundtrack. They source both pre-recorded materials, such as songs, as well as artists to create original pieces. Once the director makes the selections, the music supervisor negotiates for rights and/or commissions original tracks.

Musical. A film genre that tells a story through the songs that characters sing. Examples include *Singing in the Rain*, *West Side Story*, and *La La Land*.

Muslin. A very soft fabric which is used by the camera crew for bouncing and diffusing light.

Mute. A picture-only print that does not include a sound track.

MXF, Material eXchange Format. A digital "container" format used to store video, audio, and metadata.

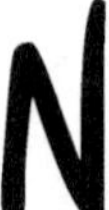

Narration. The telling of a story by an off-screen voice, identified as the narrator. In a screenplay, the narrator's dialogue is indicated by VO, or voiceover.

Narrative Device. A way by which a writer chooses to tell the story. Narrative devices are often composed of the story's tone and point of view. Some popular Narrative Devices include voice overs, flashbacks, cutaways, montages, waking nightmares, Checkov's Gun, and McGuffins, among others.

Narrative Film. A story structure following a series of dramatic events to their conclusion.

National Association of Theatre Owners, NATO. A trade organization representing the largest movie theater owners in the United States.

NC.17. A rating issued by the MPAA stating that a film contains explicit sexual or violent scenes that are not appropriate for anyone under the age of 17. Most theaters in the United States refuse to screen NC.17 films, and such rating has been described as the "kiss of death" for any film that receives it.

Negative Cost. The cost of producing a film from inception to a finished negative, before the costs of advertising, promotion and distribution are accounted for. It's the total amount of credit card debt you'll incur before getting to post.

Negative Cutter, Negative Matcher. A person who cuts and splices the negative to the final version of the film.

Negative Fill. Using a flag or a black surface to block ambient light, thereby preventing it from bouncing onto a subject; useful when shooting dark or contrasty scenes.

Negative Pick-Up. A distribution clause requiring the delivery of the finished film before an advance can be paid by the distributor. Helps mitigate the risk and ensure that a film gets delivered, and that the filmmaker isn't wasting their funds on Aspen ski-trips.

Negative Print. A reverse light image capture.

Negative Ratio. The aspect ratio of the negative.

Negative. The original film from which a positive print is made before it is edited.

Neo-Realism. A national film movement that emerged in Italy following World War II. Characterized by its focus on the lives of the poor and working-class, as well as its use of on-location filming and non-professional actors. Neo-realistic films create a raw, authentic depiction of the social and economic struggles faced by ordinary people in post-war Italy. Neorealism had a profound influence on cinema both in Italy and around the world. The movement's emphasis on social commentary and its rejection of Hollywood conventions continue to inspire filmmakers to this day. Famous examples include *Bicycle Thieves*, *Bitter Rice* and Shoeshine.

Net, Net Profit. The amount of profit after all production, salary, financing, and distribution fees are deducted from the box-office receipts or gross.

Nets. A bobbinet on a frame used to cut lighting intensity.

Network TV. A telecommunications network made up of station affiliates in different locations for the purpose of distributing content against which they can sell segments of advertising time.

Neutral Density, ND. A lens filter used to reduce the amount of light that enters the camera lens. Allowing filmmakers to use wider apertures or slower shutter speeds without overexposing the image. The ND filter functions much like a pair of sunglasses for your camera lens, they come in a range of strengths, typically measured in stops, and can be stacked or combined to achieve the desired effect.

New Deal. Changing the camera lens or position setup.

New Wave. The advent of a group of young film directors in France in the late 1950s and 60s who made films expressing their own points of view. Many of these directors began as film critics and their personal style of filmmaking was named to reflect their individual vision as the author or 'auteur' of the films. With movies like *Breathless*, *The 400 Blows*, and *Jules and Jim*, directors such as Godard, Rohmer and Truffaut influenced the growth of young filmmakers and films in late 60s Hollywood.

Newsreel. Filmed coverage of world events before there were TVs and television news. Back in the day, audiences would go to movie houses to view major world events such as both World War I and World War II. Often, newsreels were run before the feature film the audience had come to see.

Nifty Fifty, Nifty. Refers to a 50mm lens, it's nifty.

Nihilistic. A dark, depressing film that reflects the philosophy that life is without purpose or meaning. Often, a work is labeled nihilistic after the fact, perhaps by a critic; nihilism is almost an umbrella term encompassing a varied history of philosophical thought questioning the existence of morality – it is not a genre. Examples include *A Clockwork Orange*, *American Beauty* and *No Country for Old Men*.

Ninja Blade Recorder, The Ninja. A production recorder, monitor and playback deck, all in one. Who would have thought?

Nitrate Film Base. A highly flammable outdated type of film base.

NLE. Non-Linear Editing.

No Animals Were Harmed. A trademarked certification by the American Humane Association, informing audiences that animals were treated well on this production.

No Good. A call made on set to set up for a second take, something went wrong.

Noir. Short for film noir.

Noise Reduction. The process of digitally removing or suppressing unwanted artifacts in an image or sound.

Noise. Undesired electrical interference in audio or video. *See, Artifact.*

Non-Linear Editing. The process of editing a film without having it assembled first in linear sequence. Examples of non-linear films include *Pulp Fiction*, *The Social Network*, and *Memento*.

Non-Reflex. A camera in which the viewfinder is viewed via a separate lens.

Non-Speaking Role. A small, non-speaking role in a film.

Non-Sync. A scene shot without sync sound.

Non-Traditional Casting, Blind Casting. The casting of diverse actors in roles that are not defined by or limited to a specific racial background or gender identity. It's one of the many reasons that people hate *The Rings of Power* series for some reason.

Non-Union. (1) An individual who is not a union member, such as a non-union actor or extra. (2) A film in which the budget falls beneath the amount that would make it subject to union rules.

Normal Lens. A lens that reproduces a "normal" field of view as compared to longer or shorter lenses which produce an expanded or distorted field of view.

Nose Room. The space between the edge of a character's nose and the edge of the frame, in a profile, ideally.

Nostalgia Film. A film that glorifies the past.

Notes. Another term for Script Notes. Feedback provided to a screenwriter on the development of their script. These notes are typically provided by industry professionals, such as agents, managers, producers, or production company executives. The purpose of script notes is to help the screenwriter improve the quality and marketability of their script, and to ensure that it aligns with the intended vision of the production team.

Novelization. Creating a novel from a film or out of a screenplay, reversing the more typical order of basing a film on a novel. The concept is sometimes used as a marketing tool or in the case of a blockbuster movie, to satisfy the enormous, continuing interest among the movies' fans.

NTSC, National Television Standards Committee. The standard for TV/video display in the US and Canada.

Nut, House Nut. The theater's operating costs. The minimal amount of money the theater must gain from ticket sales and concessions to cover the mortgage, turn on the lights, open the doors, and run that darn popcorn machine!

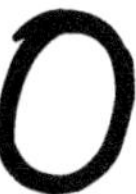

O.C.N. The film component that is exposed within the camera, representing the initial generation of an image.

Obie. A term used to describe an eye-light that is attached to a camera with the purpose of providing an actor with an eye light effect. It's what makes the actor look alive, and their eyes, interesting!

Obligatory Scene. An expected scene for a particular genre. For example, a drunk detective smoking a cigarette in a film noir, two cowboys slowly reaching for their guns in a western, and Tom Cruise jumping off an exploding motorcycle onto a moving train in every Tom Cruise movie.

Off Book. When an actor has their lines memorized and is able to perform their dialogue without the need to look at the script or call "line!" every 25 seconds.

Off Mic. A call to inform the director that dialogue was not properly picked up by the microphone. Guess we're doing that again!

Office PA, Office Production Assistant. Someone who is hired to answer phones, make copies, run errands, water the plants, and keep the production office running smoothly.

Office, Production Office. The off location setting in which producers and staff manage the business of the production and which opens before and closes up after the shoot starts and wraps. It's the place you go to cry in private when the crew won't allow you to use the crane.

Offline Edit. Editing a film with low resolution proxy files to increase performance and reduce required disk space. For when your 2015 Macbook Air is running extra slow.

Offstage, Off-Camera. Any action or dialogue occurring beyond the boundaries of the frame and not seen by the audience.

OMF, Open Media Framework. A file format intended for transferring media between different software applications on different platforms. If you want to send a project from Premiere to Resolve, better bring your OMF game.

On-Set Teacher. A teacher hired to teach the appropriate schoolwork to all school-aged minors on set, because you can't get away from doing homework, even if you're the star of *Kid Avengers 4*.

One Light Shot, Single Light Shot. A shot in which only one light source is used.

One Man Show, One Woman Show. A feature film or a short, in which there is just one performer. Examples include *All Is Lost*, *Moon*, *Wrecked*, *Buried*.

One-Liner. A one-line quip or punch line, "Frankly my dear, I don't give a damn", or "I'll cry when I'm done killing!"

One-Reeler. A film shorter than 13 minutes, or... a short.

One-Sheet. A poster or informational single-sheet publicity document, designed with original graphic art. Often used when promoting a film to distributors or foreign buyers as well as later on to advertise directly to the public.

Online Edit. Once an offline edit is complete, the low-resolution proxy is replaced with raw, high-resolution media. So, better invest in some serious hardware.

Online Editor / Offline Editors. Offline editors possess the ability to exercise creative discretion when making decisions about various elements such as shots, cuts, dissolves, fades, and more. On the other hand, online editing involves assembling the final cut of the project by editing together the high-quality footage. If you are shooting a feature on a budget, you'd likely have one editor doing both roles.

OOV, Out of vision. Dialogue is heard but the speaker is out-of-frame and cannot be seen.

Opacity. The degree of transparency in an image, recorded in the image's alpha channel, the more opaque something is, the more you can see through it.

Opening Credits. The opening credits sequence, presented on the screen before a movie begins, typically lists the production company, movie title, directors, and producers.

Opening Weekend. A critical measure of the film's success in the box office, the opening weekend refers to the first three to four days in which the film is screened to the public in theaters.

Opinion Makers, Opinion Makers' Screening. The OG influencers. People who are identified by publicists, marketers and the press as having an effect on public opinion, particularly in terms of the word of mouth that they create about a film. They are invited to early screenings and events in the expectation that they will spread buzz and create demand for tickets when the film is released.

Optical Effects. Fades, dissolves, and other visual effects created at a film laboratory.

Optical Printer. A printer used to create special effects for motion pictures.

Optical Resolution. The resolution at which a device can capture an image. Higher isn't always better, after all - how the heck do you edit an 8K resolution without your computer being set ablaze.

Optical Sound. The analog method of storing sound recordings on transparent film. Most films are still processed with both digital and analog soundtracks to ensure compatibility with any projection systems used in movie theaters.

Optical Zoom. A feature in film cameras that allows a camera to bring the image closer prior to capturing it. The greater the optical zoom of a camera, the better the outcome will be.

Opticals. Shots and effects produced through Optical Printing.

Option. A legal agreement between a producer and a screenwriter, granting a producer the exclusive right to develop and market the script before acquiring it. Producers and development executives use option agreements to represent, package, and secure funding for the screenplay's production and distribution. The gleeful screenwriter received a fee for taking their script off the market.

Orange Stick. The preferable way to clean the camera gate without scratching or damaging something expensive.

Original. The original film negative as opposed to a print.

Oscar Bait. A film that appears to have been produced solely for the purpose of garnering nominations for Academy Awards. These films are typically released towards the end of the year, just before Oscar season, in order to meet eligibility requirements and stay fresh in the minds of voters. Oscar baits often have distinct characteristics, such as lavish production, lengthy runtimes, historical period dramas, where female actors shed a single tear while a dramatic violin plays in the background.

Oscar, Oscars, Academy Awards. That award you really want to win! Best get your speech in place, just to get it out of the way.

OT. In film budgeting, OT refers to overtime hours and pay, both of which are regulated by the union. Actors get overtime when you exceed the allotted time (10 hours or 8 hours, depending on your budget).

OTS, OS, Over the Shoulder. A camera angle shot over an actor's shoulder in a dialogue as part of the scene's coverage. Medium shots are commonly used when shooting conversations.

Out point. The point at which a clip ends in the editing timeline.

Out-Take, Outtakes, Bloopers. An unused, discarded take, filmed but ultimately left out of the final version of a production due to (often comical) mistakes or errors. These may include flubbed lines, actors breaking character, on-set pranks and Will Ferrel just being himself.

Overacting. Over-the-top acting. It can be viewed positively or negatively. In some roles, particularly in comedy films, overacting is necessary to create a larger-than-life character. Overacting can also be employed to portray an outlandish character or emphasize the villainous traits of a character.

Overages. Additional profits paid to the producer by a film distributor or sales agent after the minimum guarantee (MG) has been paid off.

Overcrank. A technique in film cameras in which the frame rate of a shot is increased beyond the standard used throughout the rest of the film. Since the cinema standard frame rate is 24 frames per second, any video shot at more than 24 frames per second is typically referred to as overcranked.

Overexposure. Filming a scene with too much light, which results in the images being too bright (or, overexposed!). Generally, overexposure occurs as a result of poor camera setup or settings, so if you want someone to blame...

Overlap. A popular editing technique that carries over dialogue, sounds, or music from one scene to another.

Overture. The music that plays before the credits roll and which can set the mood for the film.

P

P&A Commitment. A contractual obligation by a distributor to spend a predefined sum on P&A (Prints and Advertising) to support the theatrical release of a film.

P&A, Prints and Advertising. Prints and Advertising refers to the cost associated with distributing a film to theaters and promoting it to audiences. Prints refer to the copies of the film that are shown in theaters, either in the form of physical film reels or digital files. Advertising encompasses all promotional activities designed to inform the public about the movie and encourage them to see it. While the cost of prints is relatively low, advertising expenses can be significant.

PA / Production Assistant, Personal Assistant. (1) A person hired to handle a wide range of tasks on set. (2) A personal assistant, someone hired specifically to aid a star, producer or director with matters that are not directly related to the production.

Pace, Pacing. The tempo and speed of dramatic action as it plays out, proceeding from scene to scene. A good editor can tell the difference between a good pace, a slow page, and a problematic pace.

Package, Packaging. The practice by an agent or producer of combining several or more clients for a project and attaching them to a production to increase its notability (and the agent's cut). When in Rome, make money!

Page-One Rewrite. A script that is considered unproducible and which is determined to need a complete overhaul – either by the original screenwriter or by another writer who has been hired to replace them.

Pages. The pages of the screenplay that constitute a particular scene and must be prepared for the next day's shoot.

PAL, Phase Alternating Line. The European color television standard.

Pan and Scan. The process of adjusting the aspect ratio of a widescreen film to fit the rectangular shape of a boring television screen or a tiny Instagram aspect ratio.

Pan, Panning Shot. Abbreviation for Panorama Shot. A camera moving horizontally along an axis to sweep across a widely spread-out vista. It's big, epic, awesome!

Pancake. A type of short apple box.

Paper Tape. A roll of tape used during film editing.

Parallax. The perceptual phenomenon that occurs when the camera is in motion and the foreground and background appear to move at different rates. The effect can be achieved in two ways, depending on the camera's setup, framing, and focal length: either the background moves faster than the subject in front or vice versa.

Parallel Editing, Cross-Cutting. A film editing technique that involves interweaving two or more scenes that occur simultaneously in different locations within the film's world. Typically, the corresponding scenes will eventually intersect or have some form of connecting action.

Parody. A comedy in which an institution or convention is mocked. Parodies typically use humor, irony, and satire to mock or criticize their subjects. Some famous parodies include *Airplane!*, *The Naked Gun*, and *Scary Movie*.

Party Poopers. A honeywagon trailer containing a portable bathroom.

Pay-to-Play. When a production company guarantees, usually to an actor, that they will be compensated whether or not they act in the film, end up appearing in it or whether or not it actually gets made. Pay or pay clauses are used in the industry to guarantee that an element or talent will be available to participate in the production, oftentimes to attract capital or other notables. No risk, no reward!

Payoff. A resolution to a dramatic narrative that has taken viewers along a complicated and at times, perplexing, or frustrating storyline. When all the conflicts and contradictions are untangled and make sense in a cohesive and satisfying way, the result is called a payoff – indicating that the difficult journey has been worth enduring to receive the payoff of a well-thought out ending.

Payola. A monetary bribe, sometimes legal (a producer needs to pay $100 to the neighbor so they stop complaining about the noise), sometimes not (A studio needs to pay $10k to an EP so to not spill the beans about their shady accounting practices).

Payroll Accountant. Responsible for managing and supervising the payroll operations of the organization, with the goal of ensuring that all employee compensation is processed in a timely, accurate, and compliant manner according to government regulations.

PC Sync. A standardized connector used to sync external flash units to cameras.

Pelican, Pelican Case. A term for hard protective cases that keep your expensive gear from breaking.

Pen, To Pen a Script. To write a script, just get it done!

Per Diem. The agreed to daily allowance that a crew or cast member may receive to cover their daily living expenses, such as food, lodging, travel, etc.

Performance Capture. A full-body Motion Capture that covers everything including the body, hands, face, and extremities. A popular tool on large productions, because the Hulk isn't going to move himself.

PG, Parental Guidance Suggested. An MPAA rating to indicate that a film's content is suitable for viewing by children, at the discretion of their parents.

PG.13. The rating by the MPAA that a movie's content may be somewhat more restrictive than that of a PG rating certificate but of less concern to producers than an R.

PGA. The Producers Guild of America (PGA) is a trade association that represents film producers, television producers, and New Media producers in the United States. PGA membership provides access to numerous benefits, such as seminars, mentoring programs, and special screenings of movies during Oscar season.

Phantom Power. The method of powering microphones directly through the camera instead of through a separate source of power. A handy tool for those who don't want to rely on their boom operator for some reason.

Photo Flood. A high-powered, screw-in light bulb. Photoflood lamps feature filaments that are heated to significantly higher temperatures than those of standard lighting bulbs.

Pickup, Pickup Shot, Reshoots. Reshooting shots or scenes after production wraps; often when editing reveals that there isn't coverage of an essential part of a scene. Pickups can save your shoot; because when you have no choice, you have no choice.

Picture Car Coordinator. Responsible for managing the usage, movement, modification, and repair of vehicles in films. They work with builders of specialized vehicles, manage a team of mechanics, and act as consultants to determine the appropriate vehicles for the film's aspects and characters. They also determine the number of duplicate versions and necessary modifications, as well as plan and implement the budget for the cars' movement, fueling, maintenance, and modification.

Picture Car. A picture car refers to any vehicle that is featured in a film. Picture cars include classic cars, vintage cars, period-correct cars, special interest cars, and stunt cars, among others.

Picture's Up. Call by the camera operator to alert everyone that the camera is ready to roll.

Pigeon. A heavy, round disc with a lighting stud.

Pillarbox. Black bars placed on the sides of the image. It is used when displaying video or film that was not originally designed for widescreen.

Pin-up Girl. A model whose mass-produced pictures see wide appeal as popular culture. (Bettie Page, Betty Grable, Dita Von Teese)

Pincushion Distortion. A type of lens distortion that causes straight lines to curve inwards towards the center from the edges, common in Telephoto and telephoto-zoom lenses. Images affected by this type of distortion can appear compressed or squeezed in.

Pipeline. The necessary stages that a movie goes through in post-production, for example VFX, Editing, Color Correction, etc.,

Pitch Deck. A document used to aid in pitching a film, usually when a producer, director or writer wants to set up the project at a production company, studio, or other source of funding so that they can develop it. Often includes a summary of the film, ideas for the cast and production team along with sample art and other visual tools.

Pitch, Audio. The frequency of audible sound.

Pitch. (1) A proposal to secure financing or support for a film. (2) The presentation of a concept for a film by its creators to potential buyers.

Pixel Aspect Ratio, PAR. The ratio of the width of a pixel to its height.

Pixel. The smallest unit of information in a digital image.

Pixilation. (1) Large, unattractive square-like pixels in an image that appear over an image as a result of scaling. (2) Pixilation is sometimes created deliberately in order to censor by obscuring an image, protecting the anonymity of a participant or hiding an exposed private part.

Plate Shot. (1) A background shot with no foreground elements. (2) The live-action footage used in CGI and visual effects.

Playback. Playing music through loudspeakers while performers dance, sing, etc.

Pay Them Out. When the Oscar programmer doesn't want to hear you speak, they nod to their counterparts, and you're being silenced while cheesy music plays you off.

Pledge Holder Agreement. A guarantee by a laboratory to a financing company to not release materials without the written consent of the financier.

Plexiglass. An economical alternative to glass, it doesn't break as easily as Candy Glass, but darn it - it looks like the real thing. Just don't go throwing people through it.

Plot Point. A significant event in the story that shifts the action in another direction.

PNG. A common image format used for lossless compression.

Point of View, POV. A direction in a screenplay or shot-list indicating that the camera should show a scene through a specific character's eyes.

Points. A share of the net-profit, promised to A-list talent to guarantee participation in the film.

Polarizer, Polarizing Filter. A piece of glass placed in front of the lens in order to control reflections, darken skies, or suppress flare.

Polyester Base. A highly durable type of film.

Portable Johns. Portable toilets available off set for the crew; because when you gotta go… you gotta go!

Positive Print. A film print created from a negative that is suitable for projection.

Post Credits Sequence. A bonus scene running during or after the end credit. Popularized by the MCU and embraced by hungry fans world-wide.

Post-Production Coordinator. A post production person responsible for supporting the post production department to ensure the smooth running of the post production process.

Post-Production Supervisor. The department head in charge of the post-production department. They consult, hire and negotiate with post-production crew and vendors, curate workflows, and create post-production schedules. Post-production supervisors may have support staff, including a post-production coordinator and an assistant, depending on the project's budget and complexity.

Post-Production, Post. The final stages of the filmmaking process, it's where the movie gets finished! Post-production includes all the work done after principal photography. Includes editing, ADR, sound design, credits, visual effects, film transfers, etc.

Practical Light, Practical. Any physical light that appears in a shot, like a bedside lamp, an overhead office fluorescent, or a candle.

Pre-Code, Hays Code. The Motion Picture Production Code of 1930. A set of rules about what was allowed or not allowed to be seen on-screen.

Pre-Production. The planning stage in a film before principal photography begins. The planning stage includes casting, location scouting, and budgeting. So... better get it right!

Pre-Roll, Preroll. (1) When a department or individual has a call time earlier than the crew call. Just make sure they have coffee. (2) A stretch of time running at the beginning of a take, used in VFX and editing purposes.

Pre-Sale. Selling a film to an agent, distributor or to an audience before it is released or complete.

Pre-Screen. To screen a film, either to producers, crewmembers, friends, or just your mom and dad, before it is released for the public.

Preamplifier. An electronic device for boosting weak audio signals.

Premiere. The first large-scale screening of a film, organized to generate publicity and to prove to people how awesome you are!

Premise. The main idea or concept behind the film.

Prequel. A film containing events preceding those of an existing work, the opposite of a sequel.

Prescoring. Recording music before a sequence is available to accompany it. Driven by imagination, not footage.

Pressure Plate. Located on the other side of the film from the gate, located inside the camera.

Preview. A movie trailer.

Previsualization Artist, Previz Artist. A designer who uses low resolution proxy models to conceptualize a VFX sequence.

Primary Grading. Color grading that affects the overall color balance of an image. See Color Grading,

Prime Lens. A lens with a single focal length as opposed to a Zoom Lens. Prime lenses tend to be sharper and faster than zoom lenses.

Principal Photography. The period of main photography of the film.

Principals. The main characters in a film.

Print Stock. Film used by the lab for making copies.

Print. A positive copy of the film intended for projection, consisting of one or more reels.

Prints & Advertising. The costs incurred by a film's distributor.

Private Investor. An individual who invests his own money in a film.

Process Shot. A shot of live action in front of a projection.

Producer. Responsible for managing the production from start to finish.

Product Placement. The way companies buy advertising space within a film for their products by signing a Product Placement contract. The filmmakers agree to show a product or logo in return for compensation, payment, or sponsorship.

Production Accountant. A person responsible for managing the money and keeping the production on-budget.

Production Assistant, PA. A person responsible for various odd jobs around set.

Production Buyer. The person responsible for purchasing supplies, equipment, and props, among others.

Production Code. See Hays Production Code.

Production Company. A company allocating resources for the production of a film, such as production space, producers, connections and funding.

Production Coordinator. A person responsible for organizing logistics, hiring crew, dealing with equipment rentals, bookings, etc.

Production Design. The film's overall design, continuity, visual look, and composition. The production designer is responsible for designing the overall visual appearance of a movie.

Production Designer. Responsible for creating and managing the visual aspects of a film. They work closely with the Director and Producer to create the design style for aspects such as sets, graphics, props, lighting, and costumes.

Production Dupe. A duplicate negative.

Production Illustrator. An artist responsible for drawing storyboards.

Production Manager. A producer working under the film's chief producer, they are in-charge of the physical aspects of the production and to keep the production on-budget, among others.

Production Report. A daily progress report summarizing what took place during the shoot and reviewed by the producers and studio.

Production Schedule. A detailed plan of the timing of activities associated with the making of a movie, of particular interest to production managers.

Production Secretary. Secretary to the production manager.

Production Sound Mixer, Sound Recordist. The head of the sound department on the set. Responsible for recording and balancing the audio captured on set.

Production Sound. Audio recorded and mixed on set.

Production Trailer. Commonly used as on set production offices, star trailers for talent, or crew offices.

Production Value(s). The overall quality of the production in terms of how good the work on the screen looks. Elements such as camera movements, colors, quality, style are all aspects of this. Ultimately, it is a judgement of how rich and textured and professional the final product appears.

Production. The general term describing the processes involved in filmmaking, from start to finish.

Profit Participation. An incentive plan introduced by producers to A-list actors and notable directors that provide a share of the film's profits in addition, or in place of, the artist's agreed-upon salary. Similar in nature to backend.

Progressive. As opposed to Interlace, Progressive scanning processes each frame as one complete image.

Projection Leader. See Leader.

Projectionist. A person who operates a projector.

Projector. A device for projecting movies on screen (film or digital).

Prologue. A brief introductory scene preceding the main action or plot of a film.

Promo. A slang term for sales promotion, often used as promo piece to describe an ad for broadcast or streaming and less so now, a physical brochure containing still photos and quotes about the film.

Prompter. A person supplying actors with the correct lines from the script if they forget.

Prop Assistant. A person responsible for the placement and maintenance of props on a set.

Prop. Abbreviation for properties. Any object that an actor touches or uses on the set, such as furnishings, fixtures, food, decorations, etc.

Property Master, Prop Master. A person responsible for buying or building the props that are used for the film.

Property. Any script that has been acquired with the intent of production.

Prosthetic Appliances, Prosthetics, Prosthetic Makeup, FX prosthesis. The process of using prosthetic sculpting, molding, and casting techniques to create advanced cosmetic effects.

Protagonist. The film's main character. A principal character in a film, series, play or work of fiction, whose actions influence the narrative and who, in turn, changes in some way to reflect what happens in the story. In classic Greek drama, the protagonist is portrayed as an instigator and usually a hero; in contrast, the Antagonist interferes with the protagonist's quest.

Proxy. A low resolution, highly compressed video file that mirrors a high-resolution master. Used in online/offline editing.

PTZ, PTZ Camera Controllers. A dedicated hardware-based camera controller provides robotic camera operators with more functionality.

Publicity Assistant. Assistant to the Publicity Director. See, Publicity Director.

Publicity Department, Advertising. The department responsible for marketing and promoting a movie in the press.

Publicity Director, Publicity Executive. A person responsible for overseeing the film's publicity campaign, which entails working with all kinds of press outlets in the hope that they will print, publish, or broadcast news items or articles about the film. Arranges for press junkets and interviews with the leading actors. Publicity Directors are also employed directly by studios to manage the overall public awareness of the corporation.

Pull Back, Pull Away. A shot in which the camera moves back, distancing itself from the subject in order to reveal the full view of and details in the scene.

Pull Down. The practice of converting 24fps film to interlaced 30 fps NTSC.

Pull Focus, Rack Focus. See Focus Puller.

Pull Processing. The process of quickly developing film quickly.

Push In. A camera move that pushes or dollies forward toward the subject of the shot. Not to be confused with a Zoom Shot.

Pyrotechnician. A person responsible for the handling and operating of pyrotechnics, they regularly handle explosives and other special effects.

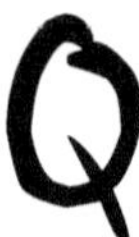

QC. Quality Control, often referred to Post-Production QC, the process of ensuring a film meets the specifications and requirements of broadcasters, distributors, and/or streaming platforms.

QRP. Quick release plate.

Quarter. A quarter of a year. Used by distribution and production companies for financial accounting.

Quartz Light. Tungsten-Halogen lights or lighting units.

Quentin, A Quentin. A closeup shot of a handsome female foot. Named so after Quentin Tarantino, who has a proclivity for female foot closeups.

Quick Release Plate. Used for quickly mounting and removing the camera from the tripod.

Quick Release Shoe. A part of the quick release plate that attaches to the camera.

QuickTime. A Cross-platform video compression software developed by Apple to support the MOV file.

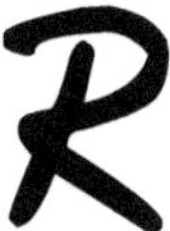

R, Restricted. A certificate issued by the MPAA indicating that persons under the age of 16 would only be admitted when accompanied by an adult.

Rack Focus. The technique of shifting the focus from a subject in the foreground to a subject in the background and vice versa.

Rack. Storage area for computer servers and other equipment.

Rating System, Ratings. Designated to classify films with regard to suitability for audiences in terms of issues such as sex, violence, substance abuse, profanity, impudence or other types of mature content. A particular issued rating can be called a certification, classification, certificate or rating.

Raw Stock. Unexposed film.

RAW, Clean HDMI. Uncompressed footage.

Re-recording Mixer. A sound crewmember responsible for balancing and mixing the final sound elements such as dialogue, music, sound effects and foley.

Re-release. The revival or rebroadcast of a work by the original distributor or studio.

Reaction Shot. A quick cut to a character reacting to the events of the scene.

Real Time. The actual time it would take for an event to occur in real life.

Rear Projection. An alternative to green screen / blue screen using real background projected onto the screen behind the actors.

Recans. Leftover film loaded into a magazine but never used.

Red Carpet. An actual red carpet is used to mark the path from curb to the theater entrance for major ceremonies such as film premieres, awards ceremonies, etc.

Red Herring. Something that misleads or distracts the audience from the plot. A plot point that leads nowhere.

Red Mags. Short for Red Cinema Camera Magazines, storage drives.

Red. Short for Red Cinema Camera. Also, a color.

Redlighted, Turnaround. A film pulled from production and abandoned by the studio. In turnaround means that another production company or studio is welcome to pay for the right to develop or produce this project.

Redrock. Manufacturer of rigs and accessories.

Reduction Print, Reduction Printing. Transferring a film to a smaller gauge (e.g., 35mm to 16mm).

Reel. A strip of film wound on a metal wheel. Attached to a projector. One reel is about 10 minutes of running time.

Reference Tone. An audio tone used to sync audio level for playback.

Reflective Light Reading. A reflective light reading measures the amount of light bouncing off the subject.

Reflex. An in-camera viewfinding system where the image in the viewfinder is viewed through the same lens that is used to photograph the image on film.

Registration Pin. Acts to steady the image during exposure. In-camera mechanism used to steady the image during exposure.

Registration. The degree to which one frame lines up with the next.

Reissue. A studio releasing a work subsequent to the original release. Similar in nature to re-release.

Relational Editing. The process of comparing shots during editing.

Release Print. A print made after the answer print has been approved.

Release. The first theatrical distribution to general public exhibition.

Remake. A new version of a film's narrative and subject matter.

Render Farm. A group of high-performance computers devoted to rendering images, used primarily to render visual effects shots and for computer-animated films.

Render. The process of outputting computer generated effects or animation for playback or final output.

Rentals. Refers to that portion of film grosses that goes to film distributors; also refers to videocassette (or DVD) rentals

Reset. Don't cut, camera and sound are still rolling. Go back to one (See "Go Back to One")

Reshoot Contingency. Funds in the budget designated for supplementary shootings, if needed.

Residuals. Money owed to a creative artist (most commonly actors, musicians, writers, and directors). Residual payments are often paid in addition to the artist's salary or original payment for the continued use of the work performed under a union contract or as an incentive.

Resolution. (1) The amount of data used to capture and play a digital file (video/audio). The higher the resolution is, the finer the detail. (2) The outcome of a dramatic sequence.

Resolver. A device that governs the speed of a tape recorder during the transfer to mag, ensuring the sound will be in sync with picture. Resolving is the process of regulating tape speed by comparing a reference signal on the tape with an external reference and adjusting the speed so that they match.

Retrospective. A tribute, exhibition, or 'looking back' at a film star's, artist's, or director's work over a span of years with a comprehensive compilation or montage of film clips or excerpts.

Reverberation. A reflection of a sound from multiple surfaces. Unlike an echo, which results from sound waves reflecting off one surface and producing a clear sound, reverberations are echoes that come from repeated or persistent reflections and so do not create the same clear effect.

Reversal film. A film that produces a positive image after exposure.

Reversal Intermediate. A second generation duplicate which is reversed to make it the same type, negative or positive, as the original. It is used for making duplicate prints in order to protect the original.

Reversal Original. A reversal film designed to be exposed in a camera.

Reverse Action. An optical effect in which the action appears backwards from its chronological sequence.

Reverse Angle Shot. A shot that is turned approximately 180 degrees in relation to the preceding shot.

Reverse Motion. The effect of running film backwards in the camera or during optical printing.

Revisionist. (1) A new, changed view of an historical assumption or given truth, often as seen through the lens of contemporary values. (2) In terms of film, a revisionist work changes the convention of a genre and retells a story so as to shake up the stereotypes of earlier generations. Westerns, for instance, have gone through several revisionist waves from their origins in the basic good cowboy vs. bad Indian trope. From Straw Dogs to Django, Unchained, filmmakers have deconstructed the once pervasive romantic myth of the American West.

Revival House. A film theater dedicated to emphasizing or specializing in only one type of film. (i.e., foreign films, older films, silent films, classics, rarely screened films, etc.)

Rewinds. A simple device for winding film, consisting of a crank and a spindle for mounting one or more reels, typically found mounted on either side of an editing bench.

RGB Color, Red Green Blue, RGB. (1) The primary colors of light, the color wheel. (2) The system by which computers and other digital devices make images and handle color information as shades of red, green, and blue or alternatively, as shades of cyan, magenta and yellow in CMY.

RGB Parade. A waveform display of the video levels for red, green, and blue components.

RGBA. A file containing an RGB image plus an alpha channel for transparency information.

Rig. A support and focus system designed to support DSLR, or digital single lens cameras.

Rigger, Rigging Gaffer. The crew member responsible for setting up the lighting and scaffolding. The rigging gaffer executes the gaffer's vision.

Right of First Refusal. A contractual agreement that gives a company "dibs" on buying rights. In simpler terms, if someone wants to sell or license their film or screenplay, and they have a "Right of First Refusal" agreement with a company, they have to offer it to that company first, on the same terms as they would offer to any other potential buyer. If the company refuses, the seller is then free to take the offer to other parties.

Rim Light. A hard backlight.

Ripple Edit. An editing technique by which adjusting the length of a clip causes clips further down the timeline to move to accommodate the change.

Riser. (1) A cylindrical metal device placed between the dolly head and the camera base to raise the camera. (2) A prebuilt platform used to raise the set, camera, or lights.

Rivas. A type of tape splicer which uses perforated splicing tape. Two models exist. One for straight cuts used for visual images, and one for the slanted cuts needed for sound.

RMS, Root-Mean-Square. A measurement of sound pressure.

Roadshow. A controversial exploitation film, heavily promoted and shown on the road.

Roll Edit. A method of shortening one clip and lengthening an adjacent one at the same time in order to maintain the original length of the sequence.

Rolling, Roll. This means that the device is recording, for example "Sound rolling," "Camera rolling."

Room Tone. Background sound (room noise) recorded on set and then used to fill in gaps when editing the sound.

Rota Pola. A polarizer, or filter, used to control glass reflections.

Rotation Shot. A complete (or half) circle spinning camera motion.

Rotoscoping. The process of tracing the outlines of live action elements for use in post-production, frame by frame. Typically used when certain elements need to be sliced out of the image.

Rough Cut. An early edited version of the film. Shots are laid out in the order they will be in the final cut but without detailed attention to the individual cutting points. While the dialogue is included in the rough cut, sound and other effects may still be incomplete or missing. Often, the music track has not been laid down. Sometimes referred to as a first cut.

Royalty. (1) A payment made to copyright holders for the use of the material they own. (2) Ongoing payments are usually called residuals or points and they are paid after the initial fees paid to an actor or director or producer for their work and only when the film makes a profit. Such payments are made on the basis of percentages that have been agreed to by contract.

Runner. Someone who is hired to run errands off set or out of the office. Usually expected to have a car and drive rather than run.

Running Time. The duration or length of a film.

Rushes. The footage that was shot during the day's shoot is then screened so that the director and other key people can evaluate what they got onto film. The footage is sometimes sent to the studio so that the executives can monitor the progress of the production.

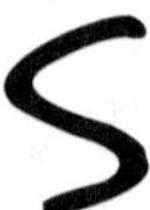

Safe Area. The specific portion of the frame indicating what will appear in the final product.

Safety Officer. Ensures the safety of everyone in the vicinity of special effects.

Safety. An additional backup take, just in case. Typically called "let's get one for safety".

SAG, The Screen Actors Guild, SAG AFTRA. The biggest actor's labor union, representing film and television actors.

Sales Agent. A person responsible for selling film rights (foreign and international) on behalf of the producer.

SAMP, Stuntwoman's Association of Motion Pictures. An honorary society of motion picture stunt coordinators, stuntwomen, and second unit directors.

Sandbag, Sand. A sand-filled cloth bag used to weigh down light stands and keep them from moving or falling over.

Sarah Jones. An invocation to remember on-set safety procedures. Sarah Jones was an AC who lost her life due to negligence on set.

Satire. A film that mocks conventionally held beliefs or practices, often with the intent that audiences will reevaluate their views about a given topic. Notable film satires include *Dr. Strangelove*, *Airplane*, *Network*, *Bullworth*, and *The Death of Stalin*.

Saturation. A measure of color depth and volume within an image. Color saturation refers to the intensity of color within the image. The higher the saturation, the more colors pop.

Scenario. A screenplay outline.

Scene Chewing. A dominating, emotional performance by an actor — often overdone and over the top – that draws all attention to that actor.

Scene-Stealing. A character whose performance draws more attention from the audience than other actors in the same scene.

Scene. A series of shots edited together to comprise a coherent dramatic event, interaction, or sequence.

Scenery. The visual environment of a shot, most often referring to a backdrop or background.

Scenic Artist. An artist responsible for the scenic painting on set, including the use of textures, colors, and surface aging.

Schedule A. Used for Day Performers.

Schedule B/C. Used for Weekly Performers, as opposed to Day Performers.

Schedule D. Used for Extra Performers.

Schedule F. A SAG contract specifying that the actor is being paid for rendered services, as opposed to a daily or weekly rate. Allows the actor to negotiate a total sum for his performance, upfront. Rates start at $6,000 a week.

Schedule H. Used for Stunt Performers.

Schedule I. Used for Airplane pilots.

Schedule J. Used for Dancers.

Schedule K. Used for Stunt Coordinators.

Schedule, SAG. In film budgeting, a SAG contract specifying an actor's daily rate, overtime, and pay on holidays and weekends.

Schedule. See Production Schedule

Scope. Another name for size.

Score. The original musical component of a film's soundtrack.

Scratch Mix, Scratch Track. A raw synch mix with no post processing.

Scratch Test. The process of checking a film for scratches before loading it to a magazine.

Scratch. Physical damage caused to a film.

Screen Actors Guild, SAG. A labor union representing film and television performers.

Screen Direction. The direction in which a character or object is moving in the frame.

Screen Test. An audition performed by a potential actor on-camera.

Screener. A promotional DVD or digital copy of a completed film sent to film critics or Academy voters to solicit reviews / votes.

Screening. The exhibition of a film in a cinema prior to its release, generally during a private event.

Screenplay. Another term for script.

Screenwriter. The person responsible for writing the film's screenplay.

Scrim. A metal filter mounted on a light to decrease its intensity.

Script Coordinator. Responsible for producing each draft of the script and annotating it for ease of use for the production team.

Script Department. A department responsible for the script of a movie.

Script Doctor. A writer or playwright hired to rewrite, polish, and improve an existing script. Whether or not they receive screen credit is determined by the percentage of their material that is used in the final movie, according to rules set by the Writers' Guild.

Script Editing, Story Editor. A process whereby a script is reviewed and changed.

Script Notes. The feedback from a producer, director or production company or studio on the draft that a writer has submitted.

Script Supervisor. A person who keeps track of the shots and continuity. They keep track of what parts of the script have been filmed and make notes on every shot.

Script. Can refer to a screenplay, shooting script, lined script, continuity script, or a spec script.

Scripty. The script supervisor

Scrub Wheel. A mechanical control for scrubbing film or magnetic tape.

Scrub. (1) Moving a piece of tape or magnetic film back and forth over a sound head to locate a specific cue or word. (2) The ability of the editing software to play back audio samples as the play head is dragged across the timeline.

SD Card, Secure Digital. Removable memory commonly found in DSLR cameras. Newer-generation SD cards include SDHC and SDXC memory cards.

SDDS. Sony Dynamic Digital Sound System. A film sound format which encodes eight tracks of digital audio outside of the sprocket holes on both edges of a film print.

Seamstress. A person who makes the costumes.

Second Assistant Camera. An assistant to the assistant cameraman. The Second Assistant Camera operates the clapperboard at the beginning of each take and loads the raw film stock or blank videocassette into the camera magazines between takes.

Second Assistant Director. The chief assistant of the 1st AD. The 2nd AD creates daily call sheets and works with the 1st assistant director to ensure a smooth shoot.

Second Banana. An actor who plays a subordinate or secondary role.

Second Lunch! Typically, a treat or meal provided between meals.

Second Second Assistant Director. An assistant to the Second Assistant Director. Responsible for directing extras, among other responsibilities.

Second Sticks. A call made to inform the 2nd assistant camera (AC) that the clap of the slate sticks was not properly captured the first time and is needed again.

Second Unit Director. The director of the second unit.

Second Unit. A team responsible for shooting scenes which do not involve the principal cast, such as stunts, inserts, crowds, scenery, car chases, or establishing shots.

Secondary Grading. Color grading that affects only a specific color range.

Segment Producer. Produces one or more single specific segments of a multi-segment film or television production.

Segment. A series of sequences that comprise a major section of the plot.

Selects. Shots selected for use before editing begins.

Senior Stand. A braced junior stand sufficiently rugged for large lights such as a 5K, 10K, or 'Big Eye'.

Senior. A 5K Fresnel lighting unit.

Sensitivity. An indication of recording or playback efficiency as might be measure of a microphone or audio tape recorder.

Sensor. A camera's sensor dictates the quality of the images it can capture. The larger the sensor, the higher the image quality. Bigger image sensors perform better in low-light situations, offer reduced noise, better dynamic range, and the ability to obtain more information.

Sepia Tone. A black-and-white image converted to a sepia tone or color.

Sequel. A movie that presents the continuation of characters, settings, or events of a previously filmed movie.

Sequence. A connected series of related scenes that are edited together and comprise a single, unified event, setting, or story within a film's narrative.

Sequencer. The hardware or software-based brain of a MIDI studio. It receives, stores, and plays back MIDI information in a desired sequence.

Serial. A multipart film that usually screened a chapter each week at a cinema.

Set Decorator. A person responsible for decorating the set with all furnishings, drapery, interior plants, and anything seen on indoor or outdoor sets.

Set Designer. The person responsible for translating a production designer's vision of the movie's environment into a set which can be used for filming. The set designer reports to the art director.

Set Dresser. A person who maintains the set per the Set Decorator's requirements, placing elements such as curtains and paintings, and moves and resets the set decoration to accommodate camera, grip, and lighting setups. Contrast with set decorator, property master. Responsible for set continuity with script supervisor and property master.

Set Dressing. (1) General decorative items in a scene that are not specifically referenced by the script or by the director as part of specific action.

Set Lighting Technician. Responsible for running electrical cables for set lighting and hanging or mounting fixtures.

Set Medic. The set medic provides for the medical needs and emergency medical logistics of the entire cast and crew and is the safety liaison between production/construction and various agencies. This person may be an emergency medical technician, paramedic, nurse, or physician. Most often the set medic is involved in the production from the beginning of preproduction or construction through filming or production through striking the set or post-production.

Set PA. A production assistant who floats around the set.

Set-Piece. Usually, a self-contained, elaborate scene or sequence that stands on its own and often necessitates complicated staging (i.e., a helicopter chase, a dance number, an elaborate fight sequence, etc.), and serves as a key moment in the film; in terms of production, it may also refer to a scene with a large set.

Set-Up, Screenplay. in screenplay terms, Setup refers to the first act in which the characters, situation, and the setting are established.

Set-Up. The place or position where the director and the director of photography put the camera (and lighting) when shooting a scene; a scene is usually shot with multiple setups and with multiple takes from each setup; aka angle.

Set. An environment used for filming. When used in contrast to location, it refers to one artificially constructed. A set typically is not a complete or accurate replica of the environment as defined by the script but is carefully constructed to make filming easier but still appear natural when viewed from the camera angle.

Setting. The time (time period) and place in which the film's story occurs, including all of the other additional factors, including climate (season), landscape, people, social structures and economic factors, customs, moral attitudes, and codes of behavior, aka locale.

Sexploitation. A non-pornographic film that features sexual themes or explicit sexual material and nudity. (The Candy Snatchers {1973}, Black Snake Moan {2006}, I Spit on Your Grave {1978}, etc.)

SGO Mistika. A high-end post-production software.

Shammy. An eyepiece chamois.

Sharp or Sharpness. Focus, used as a noun.

Sharpie. A marker useful for labeling cans of exposed rolls, labeling the slate and marking focus on the follow focus ring.

Shiny Boards. A grip reflector used for key or fill light.

Shitty Rigs! An on-set reference to the @shittyrigs Instagram page where crew members improvise crummy but useful alternatives to expensive or otherwise unavailable gear.

Shoot and Protect. A technique where widescreen footage is shot with the main action centered so as to provide easier center crop conversion to a 4.3 aspect ratio.

Shoot. The filming process.

Shooting Day. The day of filming on-set.

Shooting Ratio. The ratio between how much film was shot versus how much was used in the final version on the film.

Shooting Script. The technical script from which a movie is made.

Shop Setup. The costs of creating a shop to help construct set pieces, props and wardrobe.

Shop Steward. A person elected by the crew; on a set, a shop steward represents the crew in dealings with production management.

Shopping, Shopping a Script.

Short. A film shorter than 45 minutes.

Shortends. The unexposed remainder in a magazine that is clipped and placed back into a can for use later.

Shot Composition. The arrangement of key elements within the frame. See also shot selection.

Shot list. A list indicating the sequence of scenes being shot for the day.

Shot Lister. An iPhone / iPad application used for the creation and management of shot lists.

Shot. A single sequence of film or digital footage made by a camera and uninterrupted by an edit.

Shotgun Mic. A highly directional microphone commonly used to record production sound.

Showcard. A white artists' cardboard which is used as a reflector or for making other special rigs. It is easily cut and formed.

Shutter Priority. A metering mode in which the shutter speed is fixed, and the exposure is controlled by opening or closing the lens aperture.

Shutter speed. The amount of time it takes for the camera shutter to open and close. Faster speeds produce crisp motion and slower speeds produce motion-blur.

Shutter. A mechanism in the camera that controls the duration of transmission the light that reaches the film or sensor.

Siamese. A splitter that divides a power line into two parts.

Sibilance. An exaggerated hissing in voice patterns.

Sider. A device which cuts the light from the side of a lighting unit, usually a flag or a cutter.

Sides. The pages of a script that are given to an actor to memorize and perform for an audition, or on the day of filming.

Sight Gag, Visual Gag. an image that conveys humor visually, usually non-verbally; often used in silent film comedy, or in films with very little dialogue.

Sight Line. An imaginary line that is drawn between a subject and the object that he/she is looking at. The line of sight between a subject and the object they are looking at.

Sign Writer. The person in charge of writing and making signs shown in a production; possibly part of the set designer's team.

Signal to Noise Ratio. This is the ratio of the desired signal to the unwanted noise in an audio or video record/playback system.

Signal-to-Noise Ratio. The ratio between the desired signal and the undesired noise in a recording.

Signal. The form of variation with time of a wave whereby information is conveyed in some form whether it is acoustic or electronic.

Silent Camera. A very noisy camera, usable only for shooting silent, M.O.S. scenes.

Silent Film. A film that has no synchronized soundtrack and no spoken dialogue. Contrast with talkies.

Silent Speed. A term referring to 18 frames per second. A slightly archaic notion left over from the time when 16mm was used exclusively for home movies. It is not always that easy to find a projector that will project at 18 frames per second and so films shot at silent speed will often be speeded up slightly, whether the filmmaker intended this of not.

Silk. A material used to diffuse or reflect light.

Silver Bullet. A solution that completely solves the complicated dramatic problem within a film; the term was derived from European folklore in which only a silver bullet could kill a werewolf.

Simultaneous Cable Relay. The relay by cable of television program signal transmitted over the air simultaneously with (or effectively simultaneously with) the original transmission.

Singer. A featured vocalist: often the person who sings a film's theme song.

Single Perf. Short for Single Perforation.

Single Reel. In 35mm a reel is 1,000 feet of film (or usually a little less).

Single Source. A term used to refer to a single light source.

Single System. Single System refers to recording, editing, or projecting sound and picture together on the same piece of film. Single system has some distinct editorial disadvantages, hence the more common use of Double System for shooting and editing. Single systems are most typically used in news gathering.

Single-Stripe. Magnetic film that contains a single audio track, which is coated with oxide.

Single, double, or triple Nets. Nets are similar to flags; they are used to reduce or soften the amount of light that is striking your subject. You can add more nets to diffuse the light further.

Single. A shot with only one subject in the frame.

Size. A film element, used by the filmmaker to indicate a character's or object's relative strength compared to other things or persons.

Sketch. A short scene that typically lasts less than 15 minutes.

Skip Frame. Cutting or skipping selected frames to speed up the action.

Slapstick. A broad form of comedy in which the humor comes from physical acts or pantomime. (*There's Something About Mary, Tommy Boy, Ace Ventura: Pet Detective, Scary Movie,* etc.)

Slasher film. A subgenre of horror film, typically involving a mysterious, generally psychopathic killer stalking and killing a sequence of victims usually in a graphically violent manner. (*Halloween*, *The Texas Chainsaw Massacre*, *A Nightmare on Elm Street*, *Friday the 13th*, etc.)

Slate, Clapper. See clapboard.

Slate. The identifier placed in front of the camera at beginning of a take using a clapperboard. A clapperboard typically features take numbers and shot information.

Slave. An audio tape or videotape transport.

Sleeper. An unpromising or unpublicized movie that eventually becomes popular or financially successful beyond expectations.

Slop Print. An untimed black and white dupe print used for projection in a sound mix.

Slow Motion. A shot in which time appears to move slower than normal.

SLR, Single-Lens-Reflex. A single-lens reflex camera uses a mirror and prism system that permits the photographer to view through the lens and see exactly what will be captured, contrary to viewfinder cameras where the image could be significantly different from what will be captured.

Slug Line, Slug. A header appearing in a script before each scene or shot detailing the location, date, and time that the following action is intended to occur in.

Slug. A rather unattractive sounding name for Filler.

Slug. A strip of blank leader or image-bearing film used as leader. (Film Editing)

Slug. A strip of film or digital effect used to fill in black areas on the timeline.

Slush Pile. A set of unsolicited scripts and query letters sent to a production studio by agents and their clients.

Smart Side. Looking in the same direction as the lens, the left side of the camera

Smash-Cut. An abrupt, jarring, and unexpected change in the scene.

SMPTE Leader. Another term for Academy Leader.

SMPTE Timecode. A set of cooperating standards to label individual frames of video or film with a time code defined by the Society of Motion Picture and Television Engineers. *

SMPTE, Society of Motion Picture and Television Engineers. A film and television standards group that, among other things, standardized the use of SMPTE timecode.

Snake. A multi-channel audio cable.

Sneak Preview. Also referred to as a Sneak. An unannounced screening of a movie before the premiere. Also referred to as a Sneak and can be used as a verb, i.e., "We're sneaking it this weekend in Dallas."

SnorriCam. A camera rig that is attached to the body of the actor, facing the actor directly, so when they walk, they do not appear to move, but everything around them does.

Soft Box. A light diffuser used to reduce and/or soften light.

Soft Focus. A cinematographic effect in which a filter is placed over the lens to reduce the clarity or sharpness of focus.

Soft Light. A type of light with a built-in surface to act as a soft bounce card.

Soft Sticks. A phrase called by the clapper loader when circumstances force a tight clap, sometimes inches away from an actor's face.

Soft Tape. A cloth tape measure.

Softie. The first AC or focus puller. See AC, Assistant Cameraman.

Soliloquy. A dramatic monologue delivered by a single actor with no one else onstage.

Sony Dynamic Digital Sound. A noise reduction and sound enhancement process by Sony.

Sound Blanket. Thrown over noisy items. See Blanket.

Sound Crew. Crewmembers responsible for creating the film's soundtrack. (Sound designer, sound editor, sound effects, sound mixer, foley, boom operator, etc.)

Sound Designer. A post-production artist responsible for creating original sound elements.

Sound Effect. A sound that matches the visual action taking place onscreen.

Sound Effects Editor. Sound editor specializing in editing sound effects.

Sound Fill. See Filler.

Sound Master Positive. A sound print made for producing duplicate negatives.

Sound Mix, Sound Mixer. (1) The process of recording the production sound on the set during shooting. (2) The crew member who is responsible for this process.

Sound Negative. A negative sound image on film.

Sound Speed. 24FPS or, frames per second.

Sound Transfer. The process of transferring sound in different film formats as well as converting a mix session to the Answer Print.

Sound. The audio portion of a film.

Soundstage, or Stages. A large, soundproof structure in which productions are filmed. The stage refers to the sets that are built inside and upon which the action is filmed. Many TV shows are filmed this way.

Soundtrack. The audio component of a film, including the dialogue, musical score, narration, and sound effects, that accompany the visual components.

Source Material. (1) The original work in a non-dramatic format upon which a screenplay may be based, such as a novel, video game, or non-fiction work (a biography or magazine article). (2) Permission must be obtained to use source materials, which are often under copyright. (3) When stage plays, old films or foreign films are turned into new screenplays, the material is referred to as an earlier property that becomes an adaptation.

Source Music. Music originating from a source within the film scene such as a radio, CD, etc.

Spaghetti Western. A western filmed in Italy, many times with American leading actors. (*Django Unchained*, *The Good, the Bad and the Ugly*, *The Great Silence*, *A Fistful of Dollars*, etc.)

Sparks. A slang term for electrician. See Juicer.

Speaking Role. A speaking role in which the character speaks scripted dialogue.

Spearhead Display. Allows the color corrector to perform color adjustments in terms of lightness, saturation, and value.

Spec Script. A non-commissioned script sent to a studio or filmmaker for consideration.

Special Effects Assistant. Responsible for carrying out the instructions of the Special Effects Supervisor.

Special Effects Foreman, SFX Foreman. Supervises the Prop Shop, where members of the Special Effects Crew build the props needed to produce artificial effects.

Special Effects Producer. Responsible for planning and creating all of the SFX elements of shoot during pre-production.

Special Effects Supervisor. Responsible for designing moving set elements and props that will safely break, explode, burn, collapse, and implode without destroying the film set.

Special Effects Technician, SFX Technician. Produces visual, pyrotechnic (explosive) or physical effects to create a particular illusion.

Special Effects, SFX. On-camera effects used to create visual illusions, as opposed to those created in post-production (Visual Effects, VFX).

Special Makeup Effects. Specialized makeup.

Special Operator. A member of the Electric Department who specializes in operating lamps and generators.

Specifics. Any sound effects that directly relate to the picture.

Specular Highlights. The bright spot of light that appears on shiny objects when illuminated.

Specular. Highly directional, focused "hard" light.

Speed. A call by the camera operator or boom operator to acknowledge that they are rolling.

Spider. A term for Spreader.

Spikes. Small pieces of tape placed around the legs of a tripod before they are moved, making it easy to return things to their original position.

Spill. Unwanted light, such as green light being reflected from a green screen onto a subject.

Spin-Off. A new film or TV show derived from an existing product or franchise.

Splice. A method of joining two pieces of film so they can be projected as one continuous piece.

Splicing Tape. A special type of clear tape used to splice film.

Spline. A curve in 3D space defined by control points.

Split Cut. An edit from one scene to another in which the audio starts before or after the picture cut.

Split Screen. Dividing the screen into two or more actions with different shots in each section.

Spoiler. Information about the plot or ending of a film that may damage or impair the enjoyment of the film.

Spoof. A comedic film that pays tribute to an earlier film in a humorous way. (*Scary Movie, Young Frankenstein, Top Secret!, Walk Hard: The Dewey Cox Story*, etc.)

Spool. A roll upon which film is wound.

Spot Meter. A type of meter for taking a Reflective Light Reading.

Spot Metering. The measurement of small areas of the total picture area.

Spotting. The process of analyzing and identifying the specific scenes or points where music cues or effects cues will take place.

Spreader. A piece of gear consisting of three arms on a central hub attached to the bottom of a tripod to keep the legs from collapsing outwards.

Spring Lock. A round spring-loaded clamp that goes on the end of a rewind to allow several reels to turn together.

Sprocket. Geared wheels used to wind film through a mechanism into a camera or projector.

Spun. Spun glass diffusion material.

Squawk Box. A small speaker used to amplify

the recorded sound on an editing bench during the editing process. See Editing bench.

Squib. A small explosive device, which. when detonated. will simulate the effect of a bullet/puncture wound or small explosion. When worn by actors, they typically include a container of blood which bursts upon detonation.

Stabilization. See Image Stabilization.

Stage Box. A distribution box with six pockets for stage plug connectors.

Stake Bed. A flatbed designed to carry unusually tall cargo such as cranes, prop cars, etc.

Stand-In. A person who takes the place of an actor during the scene, light, and camera setup. Not to be confused with stunt double and body double.

Standard Definition (SD). Television broadcasting standard with a lower resolution than high definition.

Standards Conversion. The process of converting from one television standard to another.

Standby Painter. A scenic artist on standby for last minute changes.

Standby Props. Responsible for explaining how individual props work to the actors and directors.

Star System. The way in which studios groom stars under contract.

Star Vehicle. A film produced for the purpose of showing off the talents of a performer.

Star. A famous, talented, and popular celebrity.

Static Shot. A motionless shot.

Steadicam Operator. A skilled camera operator specializing in operating a Steadicam.

Steadicam. A lightweight camera mount that keeps it steady when handheld or moving.

Steenbeck. A popular brand of flatbed.

Stem. A separate audio output for a group of tracks.

Step. The act of scrolling through video one frame at a time.

Stereo. Two-channel audio combined into a single track with outputs for the left and right speakers.

Stereotyping. The act of portraying a character in offensive or distorted way.

Still Photographer. A person who photographs single stills on set to be used by the publicist.

Still. A single image.

Stinger. (1) A surprising, last-minute bit of dialogue appearing after the end or closing credits. (2) An electrical extension cord.

Stock Character. A minor character whose actions are completely predictable or stereotypical.

Stock Footage. Royalty free footage that can be licensed for use in other films. Stock footage is beneficial to filmmakers as it saves shooting new material.

Stock Music. Music not written specifically for the film in question, often licensed for use in the production.

Stock. Unexposed film.

Stop date. The last date on which a performer or director can be obliged to work.

Stop Frame. See Freeze Frame.

Storage Card. A compact memory storage device used to store data captured by a digital camera. (CF, SD, xD, SmartMedia, etc.)

Story By. A credit referring to the person who created the story or wrote the treatment.

Story Editor. A contributing writer who edits scripts, develops, and pitches stories to the studio or producer who employs them.

Story Producer. A writer/producer who may be involved in editing source footage to create and nuance story.

Story. The events that appear in a film.

Storyboard, Storyboarding. A sequence of drawings and illustrators with some directions and dialogue, representing the shots planned for a movie.

Storyliner. Responsible for creating the plot twists for a given story line.

Streamer. Used to describe someone who streams films on streaming platforms.

Strike. The process of breaking down a camera position, location or set.

Stripe. 35mm mag stock.

Studio Chief. The head or chairperson of a film studio who possesses the final authority to greenlight each film for production.

Studio System. (1) The control studios had over aspects of assembly-line filmmaking and film production from the 1920s until the late 1950s. (2) The metadata system used by Baseline Syndication, a provider of film and television metadata information. See Metadata.

Studio. (1) A company that specialize in developing, financing, and distributing feature films. (2) A site used for a film production, with physical sets, stages, offices, backlots, etc.

Stunt Car Rigger. Specialize in making any vehicle ready for stunt driving.

Stunt Coordinator. A person who arranges and plans stunts, will arrange the casting and performance of the stunt, working closely with the Director and the 1st AD.

Stunt double. A stunt performer used to replace

an actor when the scene calls for a dangerous or risky action. Not to be confused with body double and stand-in.

Stunt Driver. A precision driver used in stunt car scenes.

Stunt Gear. Equipment needed to perform stunts on set.

Stunt Performer / Stunt Player. A specialist actor who performs stunts.

Stunt Rigger. Responsible for constructing safe and efficient sets for execution of stunts.

Stunt. A dangerous piece of physical action. Often performed by a stunt performer.

Stylized. The artificial exaggeration or elimination of details in order to deliberately create an effect.

Subplot. A secondary, subordinate, or auxiliary plotline, often complementary but independent from the main plot.

Subtext. The deeper and usually unexpressed "real" meanings of a character's spoken lines or actions.

Subtitles. Captions displayed at the bottom of the screen to translate or transcribe the dialogue or narrative.

SUI. In film budgeting, SUI stands for State Unemployment Insurance. Typically found under the "Fringes" category.

Suites or "The Suits". A nickname for Studio Representatives. Someone sent to the set by the production company to represent the studio's interests.

Sundance. The Sundance Film Festival.

Super 16. A single-perforated, motion picture film that uses the maximum image area available on conventional 16 mm film.

Super 35. A motion picture film format that uses

the same film stock as standard 35 mm film.

Super 8. A motion-picture film format released in 1965 and popularized by Eastman Kodak. It was most widely used for filming home movies and amateur, low budget films in the 60s.

Super Speed. A fast prime lens, typically with a T-stop of 1.3.

Superimpose. An optical printing process that places or 'exposes' one image on top of another on the same piece of filmstock.

Superimposition. A double exposure done through optical printing, as in superimposed titles, etc.

Supervising Producer. Works on behalf of (and sometimes in lieu of) the Executive Producer.

Supervising Sound Editor. A chief sound editor.

Supporting Feature. The feature presentation. See Double Bill.

Supporting role / Supporting Cast, Supporting Actor. Actors responsible for playing secondary / supporting characters.

Surreal. A term applied to a film expressed by a random, non-sequential juxtaposition of shots that go beyond realism. (The Beyond {1981}, The Blood of a Poet {1930}, The Seashell and The Clergyman {1928}, etc.)

Surround Sound. A sound system which creates the illusion of multi-directional sound through speaker placement. See Dolby.

Survey / Survey Costs. The costs to travel and research locations.

Suspenser, Thriller. A genre that uses suspense, tension, and excitement as its main elements. (*Psycho, The Silence of the Lambs, The Sixth Sense, Black Swan*, etc.)

Sustain. The amplitude of a sound or musical

note while it is being held.

Swashbuckler. Adventure films with a heroic, athletic, sword-wielding character. (*The Three Musketeers*, *Pirates of the Caribbean*, *The Legend of Zorro*, etc.)

Sweeten. Enhancing the sound of a recording or sound effect with equalization or another signal processing device.

Swing Gang. Set dressers who dress and strike sets, as well as pick up and return the dressing.

Sword and Sorcery. A class of fantasy movies characterized by the presence of wizards and warriors, magic and sword fighting. Examples include *Jack the Giant Slayer*, *The Northman*, and *The Green Knight*.

Sword-and-Sandal Epic, Peplum Film. A genre of largely Italian-made historical or biblical epics, popular during the 60's. (*Hercules Unchained*, *Maciste in Hell*, *Demetrius and the Gladiators*, etc.)

Syd Field. Short for Syd Field's Introduction to Screenwriting. Most notable for his contribution to the "three-act structure".

Symmetry. When one side of the frame balances out or mirrors the other.

Sync Mark. The point at which the clapsticks come together after a slate is called.

Sync Rights. A license that allows a filmmaker to use a song in a feature film. Not to be confused with Master Rights.

Sync Sound. Sound recorded while shooting picture. Recorded with either crystal or cable sync to line up and not drift out of sync.

Sync. The degree to which sound and picture are lined up. Syncing is the process of matching sound and picture before editing.

Synching Dailies. Assembling, for synchronous interlock, the picture and sound workprints of a day's shooting.

Syndication. In broadcasting, syndication is the sale of the right to broadcast television programs by multiple television and radio stations, without going through a broadcast network, though the process of syndication may conjure up structures like those of a network itself, by its very nature.

Synopsis. A summary of the major plot points and characters of a script, generally in a page or two. It's "the thing" that sells movies in Hollywood, because no one likes reading anymore.

System Administrator. A person employed to maintain and operate a computer system or network.

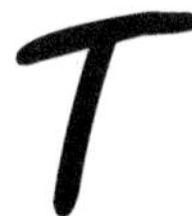

T-Stop. A true way of calculating mathematically the amount of light passing through the lens and into the sensor, different than an F-Stop — which uses the opening of the iris to assess the amount of light passing through.

T-Stops. A more accurate measurement of light passing through a lens than the commonly used F-Stop because it is taking the amount of light lost and absorbed within the lens into consideration.

Table Read, Read-through. An organized reading of the screenplay with the cast seated around the table with the director.

Tachometer. An on-camera gauge measuring the film speed while the camera is running.

Tag Line. A short, memorable line used to characterize a film in marketing, typically used in posters, trailers and commercials.

Tail Leader. A leader used at the end of a strip to indicate the end of a reel.

Tail Slate. A phrase used when marking a shot (with a clapper) after the content was shot as opposed to the beginning. The clapper will usually hold the slate (clapper) upside down and say "Tail Slate".

Tail. The end of a shot or a roll.

Take Down. Using nets, scrims, and dimmers to reduce light.

Take Down Notice. A request to remove online content that is allegedly illegal, such as copyrighted material.

Take. Multiple versions of the same scene or partial scene that have been filmed or shot digitally. The director will have the actors perform the same material until a satisfactory, usable shot or take is obtained.

Talent Agent. Agents who represent actors exclusively as opposed to Literary Agents who represent directors and writers.

Talent. Anyone appearing on-camera, the actors.

Talkie, Talkies. The colloquial term for the early films of the 1920s that incorporated sound and spoken dialogue instead of subtitles or title cards.

Talking Heads. (1) A medium shot, from the neck up, of a person talking. (2) Often refers to newscasters or TV commentators who are shown talking while seated behind desks.

Tap. The monitor hooked to the camera

Tape Grade. Color correction performed from a master tape rather than the conventional digital or film.

Tape Recorder Operator. A sound crew member responsible for operating and maintaining tape-based audio recording equipment on set.

Target Audience. (1) The potential viewers the filmmakers believe will want to see the film they hope to make and to whom the refer in order to get funding for their film. (2) Male audiences between the ages of 18-35 have been considered to be the most frequent ticket buyers who also possess great buying power for merchandise that can be promoted by a film or advertised in commercials such as cars and beer. (3) The audience that responds most favorably to a film during testing and to which marketing executives will direct their promotional and advertising campaigns.

Teamsters, The International Brotherhood of Teamsters, AFL. The labor union that began by representing drivers and truckers and which has now grown to represent a wide variety of blue-collar, skilled, and professional workers in a number of American industries as well as in the film and entertainment industry.

Tearjerker. (1) A term referring to a film with an ending that is extremely sad or tragic. (2) Originally the term came into usage in the early 1900s to describe a newspaper story that was either tragic or written melodramatically and in either case, would induce tears and sell newspapers. Tearjerker can be used pejoratively but can also describe big box-office hits such as Beaches and E.T. Contrast to and see, Feel-good film.

Teaser Trailer. A short version of the trailer released months before a theatrical release or drop from a streamer to generate excitement among potential viewers.

Tech Noir, Tech-noir. A film genre that is a hybrid form of film noir and sci-fi. Often set in a dark, fantasy world, technology is shown as an evil, destructive element. Ridley Scott's Blade Runner is considered a prime example of this dystopian genre.

Technical Advisor, Consultant. Professionals with expertise in a particular field who are hired to provide technical advice for background, character, and accuracy when a film is set in a specific milieu such as the military. Any story in which a protagonist's profession is depicted benefits from information that will enhance the visual narrative with details and portray the characters' actions realistically.

Technical Grade. A telecine transfer adjusted to be as flat as possible so as not to lose any color information.

Technicolor. A well-known color film process invented in 1916, also the name of the corporation itself, offering different high-end services to filmmakers.

Technocrane. A telescopic crane capable of producing versatile shots.

Telecine Colorist. Responsible for a Telecine Grade. See Color Grading, Telecine.

Telecine. A machine for scanning and transferring motion picture film to a digital format in real time.

Telegraph, Telegraphing. The narrative device in which an action or piece of dialogue suggests something that will happen later in the film.

Telephoto Lens. A long-focus lens in which the physical length of the lens is shorter than the focal length. This equipment serves to normalize the difference between the size and distance of near and far away objects and it allows the camera operator to bring distant objects closer into view. The telephoto lens is especially common in wildlife photography.

Teleplay. A script written for a television show.

Television Movie. A feature-length movie produced expressly for television and not for a big-screen, theatrical release. Sometimes known as a Movie-of-the-week or MOW.

Television Rights. The legal permission or rights that are sold to a distributor, usually a network, to broadcast the specific property on TV.

Television Series Pilot, TV Pilot, Pilot. (1) The first episode of a series. (2) A pilot may be "ordered" by a network to determine whether they want to commit the funding to produce a first season. (3) A pilot can be aired to generate audience feedback before producing subsequent episodes.

Television Special. A television production of a singular or newsworthy event, usually an hour or two hours in length or in several one or two-hour episodes. It is a limited project and not ongoing like a series.

Television Spot. A short TV advertisement space of between 15, 30 or 60 seconds. A commercial.

Telewriter. An archaic term for a screenwriter.

Temp Dub. The first round of mixing dialogue, music, and sound effects.

Temperature. Temperature refers to the color of light and how warm or cool it appears.

Tenner. A colloquial term for a Mole-Richardson 10/12K 24" Big Eye Tener Fresnel light.

Tentpole, Tentpoles. A film or series of films, usually self-contained stories that because of their box office success, generate sequels. Often, they are connected by a continuously featured character. Most commonly, tentpole films are produced in one of two genres – action, such as the Bourne movies or comic-book based live action, such as the Marvel Cinematic Universe films. Tentpole works are highly sought since their distributors or studios rely on the likeliness of this revenue to put out other, possibly more risky pictures.

Terra-Flite. A cross between a Steadicam and a Louma crane. See, Steadicam, Louma crane. Terra-Flite is a combination of a Steadicam and a Louma crane - it's like a superhero that can fly and hold a camera at the same time.

Tests. Film, camera, and makeup tests taken during pre-production.

The Black List. List of unsold scripts that have been widely admired as well as evaluated by an organization founded expressly to call attention to these available properties.

The Call. The various directions spoken by the director to begin a take such as "Roll Sound!" "Roll Camera!" "Mark it!" "And... Action!"

The Industry. Another name for the film or entertainment business.

The Slate. (1) Another name for a clapperboard. A fancy contraption that helps filmmakers keep track of their shots and make sure all their audio and video is in sync. (2) A production company or studio's list of upcoming projects, some of which may be in development and others in the process of production or post-production.

The Trades. The three principle daily trade newspapers that cover industry news. Often published digitally, they have been integral to the movie business since its earliest days. The big four trade magazines include *Deadline*, *IndieWire*, *Variety* and *The Hollywood Reporter* (aka The Reporter).

Theatre. The Film House of Worship - A holy place where movie-goers gather to worship their favorite flicks, it's where films are screened, presented, or viewed.

Theatrical Rights. A right granted to a distributor to give the film a limited or wide release in cinemas. It's every filmmaker's dream come true.

Theatrical. Referring to a theatrical release, meaning that the film appears in movie theaters first and exclusively before it can be streamed or televised.

Theme Music. The musical equivalent of a movie's signature fragrance. The recurring, signature part of a motion picture's score that is usually included in the opening and/or closing music.

Theme. The central, unifying concept of a film. It's described as "the heart of the story". A theme is meant to evoke a universal human experience and can typically be explained in a single word or short phrase. Common screenwriting themes include Good vs. Evil, Coming of Age, Humanity vs. Technology, etc.

Thin raster. A wide image "squeezed" by a digital camera to preserve bandwidth and then "unsqueezed" for playback, mimicking an anamorphic look for those of us who can't afford an anamorphic lens.

Three Act Structure. An outdated literary model used in narrative fiction that divides a story into three parts, the three acts. The first part is the Setup, where we meet the characters and get a taste of the world they live in. The second part is the Confrontation, where things get real and the characters face challenges. Finally, there's the Resolution, where everything comes together, the pieces of the puzzle fall into place, and we find out what happens. Popularized by Syd Field in his book "Screenplay: The Foundations of Screenwriting".

Three-shot. A medium shot framing three people.

Thriller. A film genre that will have you on the edge of your seat with mystery, suspense and unexpected twists.

Thumbnails. Small images used to reference film clips on the camera or at the editing station.

THX. A sound system for theatrical film exhibition.

Tie-in. A cross-promotion venture between a film distributor/production company and a company in which both are the same deal to create additional income and promote both products, for example a video game based on a film or a McDonalds happy meal selling action figures, etc.

Tier 0, 1, 2, 3. An IATSE term to describe a film shot for under $2 million (0), under $6 million (1), $10 million (2), and $14 million (3).

TIFF. (1) Tagged Image File Format popular for delivering sequence shots for VFX. (2) Toronto International Film Festival, a showcase of the latest and greatest films from around the world.

Tiffen. Manufacturer of filters and Steadicam gear.

Tight On, Tight on the Lens. A close-up shot.

Tilt shot. A vertical camera movement on a fixed horizontal axis. Also known as tilt pan, tilt up or tilt down.

Time Base Signal. A signal recorded for synchronizing film and sound workprints.

Time Code. Electronic guide track providing an accurate time reference and synch for editing.

Time Lapse. A cinematography magic trick to capture a series of frames over a period of time, resulting in the creation of the illusion of speed. When played back at normal speed, slow actions – such as the movement of clouds – appear to occur much more quickly than they would in real life.

Timed Print. A print where the Timer has gone through and timed every shot.

Timeline. The representation of time. In non-linear video editing, this is where you line up all your clips to create a seamless story. Think of it as a colorful, digital version of a paper timeline.

Timer. A color wizard who makes sure that every frame of your film looks as vibrant and beautiful as it should.

Timing Report. A list of notes created by the timer.

Tint. Adding a splash of color to a scene to give it a mood, like putting on a pair of colored glasses.

Title Cards. Little bits of text that pop up during a movie, like signposts along the way to help you understand what's happening and who it's happening to.

Title Design. The art of making movie titles look cool, like a street artist turning words into works of art.

Title Search. A legal scavenger hunt to make sure someone else hasn't already claimed the same title for their movie.

Titles. All the various credits that show up at the beginning or end of a movie, like a roster of the A-Team that made it all happen.

Tix. Abbreviation for tickets. Tiny pieces of paper that grant you access to a world of imagination on the big screen.

Tonal Range. The number of shades between the lightest and darkest areas of an image that a particular camera can produce.

Tone. The intended atmosphere of a film scene. The "mood" that a film scene is trying to set, like the soundtrack to your emotions as you watch the movie.

Toon. Abbreviation or slang for cartoons. The wacky, wily, and wonderful world of animated characters!

Topline. The grand poobah of credits, the one who gets top billing! They're the ones who have everyone talking about their name before the title even starts!

Tour De Force. A performance by an actor so mesmerizing, so breathtaking, so over-the-top that you'll forget it's not real!

Track. A single audio component or channel.

Tracking Shot. A shot that's always on the move, following the action like a camera operator who's been mainlining caffeine!

Trademark. A highly recognized, personal touch or style of an actor, director, writer, or musician. It's that special sauce, the secret ingredient, the unique touch that sets one artist apart from the rest!

Trades. The collective name used to refer to professional trade magazines in the entertainment industry.

Trailer. A sneak peek into the coming attraction. Think of it like a movie appetizer, it's just enough to whet your appetite and leave you wanting more!

Trainee. A crew member who is a part of the DGA training program, he or she works under the supervision of DGA members on set.

Trainer. A person responsible for training performance animals.

Transfer. Film transfer to a different format such as digital or DV.

Transition. A style of gradually changing from one shot to the other, usually by using a "transition effect" such as a fade, dissolve, wipe, etc.

Transportation Coordinator. Responsible for managing and coordinating the transportation of cast, crew, and equipment during filming.

Trash film. A low-budget film created to repel the audience by showing extremely gory shots or extremely infantile humor. Often, these movies are so bad they're good! Think of it as the cinematic equivalent of a car crash - you can't look away!

Travel & Living. In film budgeting, the cost of hotel and airfare. This category covers everything from hotel rooms to airfare, AirBnb to Priceline.

Travel Coordinator. Responsible for planning, coordinating, and booking flights, hotel rooms, rental cars, and other forms of transportation for cast and crew.

Traveling Matte Shot. A matte shot requiring intense masking since the object is constantly in motion.

Travelogue. A film that shows scenes from foreign, exotic places

Treatment. A detailed literary summary of the film's script consisting of a detailed summary of action and characters in the film. Often used to market and/or sell a film project or script. It's perfect for selling the project to a bunch of Hollywood big shots who appreciate a good story.

Trilogy. A trifecta of cinematic excellence! Imagine a story that spans three films, each one building on the previous, until the final installment delivers a breathtaking conclusion! Famous examples include *The Lord of the Rings*, and *The Dark Knight* trilogy.

Trim Bin or Editing Bin or Bin. A bin on wheels in which the film is hung while editing.

Trims. Short portions of scene-leftovers, usually a foot or less stored in their own vault box or in a trim book.

Triple Threat. An insanely talented actor or actress who can either sing, dance and act or act, direct and write.

Tripod Head. The top portion part of the tripod to which the camera is mounted.

Tripod. A support or stand for a camera, telescope, etc.,

Trombone. A device used for suspending lights from set walls.

Trope. A familiar pattern or theme that pops up again and again in movies, making us go "Oh yeah, I've seen that before!" For example, the "Damsel in Distress" or the "Bad Guy with a Heart of Gold" trope. These tropes can be both a blessing and a curse, adding predictability to the story but also giving us a good laugh and a warm, fuzzy feeling inside.

TTL, Through The Lens. A feature which measures light levels in a scene through the camera's lens, leaving the old-fashioned metering windows in the dust.

Tungsten. The shining star of artificial lighting. With its glowing color temperature of 3,200K, it's the perfect choice for creating a warm and inviting atmosphere

Turnaround, In Turnaround. When a studio puts a movie project on hold. This could be due to a variety of reasons such as budget constraints, creative differences, or simply losing interest. Producers are often free to pitch the idea to other studios and see if they can get it back on track.

Turret, Multi-Turret. A rotating powerhouse mount that can accommodate several additional lenses to be attached to the camera. Transforming your camera into a lens-swapping ninja!

TV Safe. Marked area of a frame which are pre-defined to appear on an average home television set after a film has been transferred in a telecine.

Twist, Plot Twist, Ending Twist. The curveball of storytelling that keeps audiences on their toes and keeps them guessing until the very end. It's the "Oh snap!" moment that leaves viewers pleasantly shocked and eager for more.

Two-Hander. A story driven by only two characters.

Two-Reeler. A film lasting a little over 20 minutes

Two-Shot. A medium close-up shot of two subjects, usually framed from the chest up.

Typecasting. When an actor or director's previous work is used as a catalyst in a hiring decision on a new project. A typecast artist is only hired within the confides of a certain genre where they are expected to perform well. For example, Sharon Stone and Adam Sandler were typecast in sexually explicit and slapstick comedies, respectively.

U

U-matic. An outdated analog recording videocassette format.

Ultra Bounce. A highly versatile, lightweight fabric providing a soft bounce light.

Ultrasonic Cleaner. Think of it as the Mr. Clean of the film world. This cleaning device uses high-frequency sound waves to blast away dirt and grime, ensuring that your film is spotless before printing or transferring to video.

Ultrasonic Splicer. An advanced film splicing machine. It uses ultrasonic signals to fuse film together, creating seamless splices that are almost undetectable.

Umbrella. It's like a giant, protective canopy for your film company. This type of insurance covers claims that go beyond what your regular policies can handle, so you can feel safe and dry no matter what kind of stormy waters you find yourself in. Also, you use it when it rains.

Uncredited role. A distinctive but not leading part, played by a major or minor star who has agreed or requested to not be credited. Not to be confused with a cameo. One example is the role in *Four Rooms* played by Bruce Willis.

Underacting. A natural, unself-conscious performance that is so life-like that it makes it seem like the actor is just speaking normal dialogue instead of memorized lines.

Undercrank. The slowing-down of a camera's frame rates to produce faster motion.

Underexposed, Underexposure. When there's not enough light hitting the camera's sensor, you end up with blurry, dim and noisy images that are far from the masterpieces you envisioned.

Underground Film. A movie that's as low budget and bare bones as a 99-cent burger. These flicks are made by a gang of friends who know nothing about the film industry, except for the fact that they love movies. They pitch in and do everything from acting to operating the camera, without even thinking twice about their lack of experience. Frequently associated with the films that were produced by Andy Warhol at his factory. Examples are John Waters' *Pink Flamingos*, David Lynch's *Eraserhead*, and Andy Warhol's *Blue Movie*.

Underscan. A mode in cameras and monitors allowing full view of the screen, including cropped portions. So if you're in need of a little extra screen real estate, you know what button to press.

Underscore. The music that is run underneath a section of dialogue or narration to intensify the emotion of the scene. Adding an extra layer of emotion to every scene without ever stealing the spotlight.

Union Tier. The great equalizer of the film industry. Union wage rates determined by the total budget of a film. Higher budget means higher wages.

Unions. The champion of the creative and technical forces in the motion picture industry. These professional organizations represent the little guys and gals, fighting for their rights and ensuring they get paid what they're worth. Think of them like the Justice League of the film world, taking on the big bad bosses and making sure everyone is treated fairly.

Unit Base, Base Camp. This is where you'll find everything you need, from makeup and costumes to parking and catering. It's like a giant movie-making village, with everything a filmmaker need all in one place. A

Unit Nurse, Key Set Medic. Set medics working to ensure the safety and well-being of actors, stuntmen, and fight choreographers. While the actors are jumping from buildings and fighting off aliens, the Unit Nurse is there to make sure they don't die.

Unit Production Manager, UPM. The ringmasters of the film production circus, juggling schedules, budgets, transportation, and a whole herd of below-the-line crew members. These managers are essential to the success of a film. They're the leaders with the communication skills of a diplomat, the organizational skills of a ninja, and the people skills of a psychologist. They keep the crew happy, the schedule on track, and the budget in check, and often - they're the first credit at the end of the movie.

Unit Publicist. An anxious and hardworking member of the publicity department who covers press and cultivates media exposure, reporting to the publicity director.

Unsolicited Materials. A script, idea, or other artistic material submitted to a studio or distributor without a specific request being made, or without the use of an attorney, agent, or production house. Hollywood has a strict policy of not accepting any unsolicited works, to shield themselves from any legal tussles in the event that their future projects happen to look similar to your submission.

Unspool. To screen or show a film.

Unsqueezed Print. A corrected Anamorphic print.

Up-conversion. Converting SD footage to HD format.

Upright Moviola, Moviola. A once revolutionary editing device when it was invented in 1924. It was the first motion picture editing workstation that allowed the editor to study the shots and view the footage while editing. Mostly, it has been replaced by flat-bed machines and software.

Utility Person. An assistant responsible for various manual tasks on-set.

Utility Sound Technician. A member of the sound department, most often in charge of pulling cables and dealing with technical audio issues on-set.

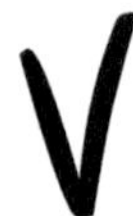

V-Mount. Referring to a V-mount battery, or V-mount lock due to the V-shaped connection piece at the back of the batteries.

Vamp. A sexually alluring female character, typically a heartless, man-eating seductress. She's the mastermind behind some of the most intriguing and alluring scenes in film history, always leaving hungry male audience wanting more. In other words, Megan Fox.

Variac. A versatile solution for altering the voltage of alternating current (AC) electricity.

Variety. Ah, Variety, the OG of the entertainment world! This daily publication was once the king of the stage, covering everything from vaudeville and variety acts to the latest Broadway productions. And now, in its digital form, it remains one of the most important "trades" in the industry, keeping everyone informed and entertained.

VariSpeed, Pitch Control. An effect in which the speed of the camera is changed mid-shot.

Vault Box. A box designed to keep your precious rolls of film safe, secure and organized.

VCR. A Video-Cassette Recorder.

Vertical Interval, Vertical Blanking Interval, VBI. The microscopic time difference between the final line of one frame and the beginning of the next.

Vertigo Effect, Dolly Zoom. A cinematic technique that distorts perspective by moving the camera towards or away from a subject while adjusting the zoom lens. This creates an unsettling visual effect, making the background seem to change size relative to the subject. First conceived by Alfred Hitchcock and successfully executed in the film Vertigo, it's since been used in numerous films like *Jaws*, *Goodfellas*, and *The Lord of the Rings*. The dolly zoom can amplify emotions, represent vertigo, suggest character realizations, and create tonal shifts, making it a versatile tool for filmmakers.

Video Assist Operator, VAO. The person responsible for setting up the Video Village, the epicenter of a film set. The VAO ensures that all video monitors are placed in the right spot for the director to have an eagle-eye view of the shot, so they can oversee the framing, focus, and overall quality of the shot.

Video Village. The lively hub of the film set. It's where the director, the DP (Director of Photography), the producer, and other key personnel gather to monitor the shot. It's like a mini-football stadium for the director's team, and the VAO is the quarterback.

Video Cassette Recorder. A device from the past for recording and playing prerecorded video tapes.

Video Master. A form of a deliverable file. It's the final, polished version of a video that's ready to be shown to the world.

Video. An analog or digital visual image.

Videographer. Another name for camera operator. When the two are credited separately, it generally refers to the person in charge of handling video cameras on-set, most likely the BTS (Behind the Scenes) camera crew.

Viewfinder. The view of the camera operator, or what the camera operator looks at in order to control the frame, focus and motion of the camera. Viewfinder can also refer to a direct-optical, EVF or LCD screen, among others.

Vigilante Picture. Call it revenge, justice, or simply a sweet, sweet payback. This sub-genre of action films features an everyday hero who takes matters into their own hands to right a wrong and deliver a good old fashioned butt-kicking. Think *John Wick* meets *The Equalizer*.

Vignette. A masking device use to darken the edges of a frame and direct the eye to the center of the frame. It's like a chic frame around a piece of art, only in this case, the art is moving.

Vimeo. A video-sharing website that is popular among indie filmmakers and often used as a platform for audition tapes by actors.

Vision Board, Mood Board. A collection of inspirational images, videos, and quotes, like a virtual vision of your future Pinterest board. It's used to get a feel for the mood and atmosphere of a film in its early stages of conceptualization.

Vistavision. A high-quality, widescreen 35mm film format with relatively low noise and grain. Vistavision is perfect for filmmakers who want to show off their cinematic skills and make a big impression.

Visual Effects Editor. An artist working to incorporate visual effects into live-action sequences and preparing them for review by the Visual Effects Supervisor.

Visual Effects Producer. The artist who turns "this can't be done" into "how the f**k did they do that?" They're the ones who take a look at the script and give the director the "how-to" guide for capturing the live-action footage, also known as "the plate". Basically, they turn a simple script into an epic visual journey.

Visual Effects Rigger. The puppet master of the VFX world, they bring characters to life by rigging them up with clicks of a button. They work to prepare animation rigs for characters, and make sure they move just like a real person (but better). Just don't confuse them with a Special Effects Rigger, who deals with more practical, physical effects.

Visual Effects Supervisor. The supervisor in charge of the entire VFX department. The captain of the VFX ship, they lead the crew and oversee all aspects of the VFX process.

Visual Effects. The magical spells cast upon a film to transform it into a visual feast for the eyes. VFX, as the cool kids call it, is the process of taking raw footage and adding some sugar, spice, and everything nice to it in post-production. From fixing minor blips to creating entire worlds and creatures, Visual Effects has come a long way from its humble beginnings and is now the glue that holds together many of our favorite movies, as well as Henry Cavill's mustache.

VITC, Vertical Interval Time Code. The little black-and-white bars that are the ninja assassins of time-coding, silently keeping track of the time while you enjoy the film. VITC is a type of SMPTE timecoding that makes it possible to sync up the sound and image in post-production. No more hand claps and finger snaps to get the timing right, VITC takes care of it all.

VO, Voice-Over, Voice-Over Artist. The voice that whispers in our ear while you're trying to watch a film, adding depth, context, and a dash of drama. Voice-Over refers to the practice of adding narration, dialogue, or sound effects to a film without the person speaking appearing on-screen. From grand epic tales to silly animated comedies, VO is the secret ingredient that brings life to a film, and Beatrix to Bill.

VU Meter, Volume Unit Meter. The traffic cop of audio signals, keeping the sound levels in check and ensuring the audience doesn't blow out their eardrums.

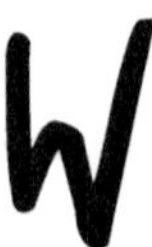

W/C. In film budgeting, the abbreviation for Workers Compensation and its cost. It's the cost for taking care of your crew in case of any on-set mishaps, it's also the law, so don't try to get around it.

Walk-On, Walk-In. The bit-part roles of the acting world, typically reserved for friends, family, pesky lottery winners and your investor's 20-year-old girlfriend. These minor roles have no lines, so no need to worry about them ruining your scene.

Walk-Through. The first dress rehearsal. It's the first time everyone gets to shut up and listen to the director talk about how their scenes will come together on location.

Walkie Check. The "Can you hear me now?" moment of radio communication! A quick check to make sure everyone's radios are working properly.

Walkies. Short for walkie talkies, these trusty devices keep everyone in communication on set and will always go off in the absolute worst moment.

Walla. A murmur sound effect, used to create the illusion of a bustling crowd on location.

Wardrobe Truck. The rolling walk-in closet of the film industry! This truck or van is used to transport all the wardrobe to and from location, from superhero suits to medieval garb and skinny jeans.

Wardrobe, Wardrobe Department, Wardrobe Supervisor. The fashionista's paradise! The department responsible for wardrobes on set and the head of said department.

Water Truck. A specialized truck equipped for washing cars, trucks, and trailers, as well as for wetting down roads to produce an awesome reflective effect. It's every cinematographer's wet dream, get it?

Waveform Monitor. The nerd's best friend! An oscilloscope used to measure and monitor video and audio levels.

Weapons Master, Armourer. The musketeers of the film world! The very important crew member who specialize in (and is responsible for) weapons, armaments, and firearms.

Wedges. The literal building blocks of a film set. Wood wedges are used for leveling and stabilizing platforms and equipment on set, or to keep doors from closing / opening all the way.

Weekly Performer. A SAG term that defines a weekly rate compensation to an actor or performer, as opposed to a Day Performer.

Wescott. A type of lighting fixture.

Western Dolly. A plywood dolly used as a camera dolly for smooth surfaces.

Wet-Gate. A process of removing dust, dirt, and hair from the film. Don't try it yourself! Please.

Whip Pan. A very fast pan. A trademark of director Wes Anderson and those who are "inspired" by his work.

White Balance, WB, Color Balance. The camera's ability to automatically correct color cast, adjusting its settings to reinterpret the color white. Just don't ask your DP about it, lest you get slapped in the face.

White Noise. A random signal with a consistent amount of energy per hertz.

Whodunit, Who Done It. A classic mystery genre of film featuring detectives with short-term memory loss who need to remind themselves "who did it?" every 5 minutes.

Whoop-Whoops. A little extra sprinkling of magical sound effects to make the sound more enjoyable and pleasant to the ear, like adding frosting to a cupcake.

Wide Lens. The clown car of camera lenses! With a shorter focal length than its counterparts, it captures a bigger slice of the scene and adds an epic, adventurous feel to your shots.

Wide Open. The lens equivalent of singing at the top of your lungs! When you set your aperture to its widest setting, you're letting in all the light to the sensor, creating a brighter shot as a result.

Wide-Angle Shot, WS. A shot captured with a wide-angle lens.

Widescreen. Any aspect radio greater than 4.3 (1.33:1) in which the image is significantly wider than it is tall. Making it perfect for capturing sweeping landscapes or dramatic action scenes.

Wild Line, Wild Sound, Wild Track. A non-sync sound, recorded separately from the movie to supplement synch takes.

Wilhelm Scream. The iconic battle cry of cinema! This distinctive scream has been used repeatedly in countless films and is sure to add a touch of classic Hollywood to your productions.

Wipe. A commonly used "push" transitional effect, most commonly used in the Star Wars films and your great uncle's wedding video.

Word of Mouth. The unsung hero of film marketing. his powerful element can make or break a film's success and it's all about what the cool kids are saying on social media.

Workprint. Another term for Rough Cut.

Workstation. Referring to any audio/video recording and editing system, even the one in your house basement.

Wow and Flutter. The funky measurement of 'frequency wobble,' a playback irregularity caused by speed fluctuations during recording.

Wow. Pitch variations sound effect, used to mimic the flutter artifact produced by gramophones and old tape recorders.

Wrangler, Animal Wrangler. The experienced animal whisperer who is in charge of the cuddly creatures on set. Whether it's a horse, a dog, or a dragon, this skilled handler ensures that all non-human cast members are treated with love and care.

Wrap Party. A joyous celebration where the cast and crew say goodbye to the cameras and hello to the after-party. It's like the prom of the film world, but with a lot more vodka.

Wrap!, It's a Wrap!, Wrapped. (1) The announcement that shooting is over for the day and it's time to grab a drink and dance the night away. (2) A statement that the shoot has ended, whether it's a shot, a scene, a character, or the entire movie.

Writer. The humble and often underpaid heroes of the film world, writers are like magicians who bring your favorite stories to life on the page, with nothing but their wits and a pen. They work their magic whether it's a novel, a screenplay, or a TV show, but somehow seem to get forgotten in most VFX-heavy blockbusters. But don't worry, they're still out there, making the world a better place one word at a time.

Writers Guild of America or WGA. A union of writing superheroes who fight for the rights of film, TV, radio, and new media writers, ensuring that every script is treated with the respect it deserves. Major production companies and studios must bow down to the WGA and hire its members, a bittersweet victory to cocaine addicts everywhere!

Written By. A credit referring to the strange person who wrote both the story and the screenplay.

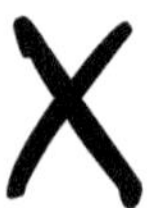

X rating. A predecessor to the MPAA's NC-17 Rating; it's the "wild child" of film ratings. Created in the 60s and retired in the 90s when the XXX symbol took over the adult film industry.

X-Y Pattern. A duo of stereo microphones that work together like Batman and Robin, positioned and aimed in crossed directions to feed two channels for stereo pickup. Perfect for capturing every nuance of your audio.

X. The secret signal that lets actors know exactly where to stand, like a lighthouse guiding ships to shore.

XD Cards. A small old-school memory card format used in older digital cameras.

Xeen. A Rokinon cinema lens brand that'll make your footage sparkle like a diamond, perfect for making your film shine.

Xenon. An extremely bright, high-intensity, non-incandescent, non-halogen lamp that shines brighter than a supernova.

XLR Connector. A standard sound connector used in professional audio.

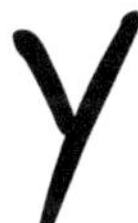

Yarn. Slang for a fabricated story with little concern for the truth; like a fairy story for adults.

Yawner. A movie that's so slow and boring, you'll need a map and a compass just to find the climax.

YMC. Acronym for Yellow, Magenta, and Cyan, one of the two ways that design and film professionals refer to how colors combine, mix, and interact. A brilliant combination of colors that are the building blocks of a beautiful design, like a rainbow in your hands.

YouTube Content Creator. A YouTube community offering help and strategies to filmmakers who want to make a living on YouTube.

YUV. A mysterious color space used in NTSC and PAL broadcast video systems.

Z

Z-Brush. A magical VFX app that lets you bring your wildest 3D-model dreams to life with stunning realism and detail - like a digital Willy Wonka for artists.

Z-Movie. A cinematic masterpiece that's the black sheep of the movie world, often boasting more laughs than a Hollywood blockbuster and a budget smaller than your grandma's pension.

Zeiss. A lens wizard that's conjured up some of the best camera lenses on the indie market (CP.2, CP.3); every indie cinematographer's wet dream.

Zero Cut. A method of cutting film negative for blow up. Each frame is given "handles" to keep the registration pin from engaging with the splice. This film editing technique is most commonly used when a lab blows up film from 16mm to 35mm.

Zone A. The COVID-Free Zone. Any perimeter within which activity occurs without physical distancing or the use of PPE. No one can be allowed access to this Zone unless they have been tested for COVID within the last 24 hours. Zone A personnel should be tested three times a week at a minimum.

Zone B. Everywhere the production has a footprint that is not Zone A. Use of PPE and stringent physical distancing practices are observed and enforced within Zone B. People working in Zone B should be tested at least once a week. Just don't get caught without your mask on or Tom Cruise will scream at you!

Zone C. Any location outside the physical set. It's wherever people employed in the production go when they're not working. Just remember to keep your distance!

Zone, The Zone System. A COVID-19 measure employed by unions to keep cool cats on set safe from the dangers of COVID. Just follow the rules and you'll be fine.

Zoom Lens. The Focus Flexer! A variable focal length lens, as opposed to a fixed local length lens.

Zoom Shot. A Zoom Shot is like that time you accidentally walked in on your roommate - it gets bigger or smaller quickly and you never know what you're going to see! Except instead of your roommate, it's a shot taken with a fancy pants zoom lens that can adjust its focus length like a boss.

Zoom. A field recorder used by indie sound mixers. The perfect tool for capturing audio on the go. Whether you're out in the wild, on a busy street corner, or in a dimly lit night club, the Zoom has got you covered.

Zoopraxiscope. An early movie device that produces animated projections, it is considered the granddaddy of the modern movie projector.

Zoptic Special Effects, Front Projection Effect. A camera system your filmmaker grandfather used before the popularization of CGI and computer-based graphics. Zoptic was first introduced during the 1978 *Superman* shoot, developed by mad scientist Zoran Perisic.

Epilogue

And that's a wrap! You've just taken a whirlwind tour through the star-studded alleys of the *Ultimate Filmmaking Term Pocketbook Glossary*—from the technical twirls of "Aperture" to the zesty zing of "Dolly Zoom."

But don't just pocket this little book (get it?) and let it collect dust next to lost candy wrappers and that "Jurassic Park" coffee mug you never use. Let it be your secret handshake into the cool club of cinema craftsmen and women, the wand that turns bewildered bunnies into confident creators.

Sure, the silver screen is full of dreams, but it's the dreamers—like you, yes you!—who keep it flickering. The set is a funhouse, a playground where stories unfold. So, keep this guide close; its pages are steeped in the magic potion that turns "What's that thingamajig?" into "Hand me that C-47! (wow, the confidence!)."

As you step onto set with this glossary in your pocket, know that you're part of a tribe of passionate, peculiar, and positively prodigious people. Keep your head high, your slate clean, and your spirit ready for adventure. Lights, camera, learn—and let the good times roll!

You're making history.

www.ingramcontent.com/pod-product-compliance
Lightning Source LLC
Chambersburg PA
CBHW051445050726
47593CB00005B/1930